THE 80
MOST COMMON
MISTAKES
IN SPANISH

THE 80
MOST COMMON
MISTAKES
IN SPANISH

FRAN GARCÍA

First paperback edition: October 2023.

Written by Fran García.

Editor and Publisher: Fran García.

Interior Design: Saiqa Falak.

Cover Art: Noemi De Feo.

Contents

"To my mum and grandma, who instilled a passion for reading in me. To my dad, for his unwavering support. To my students, who inspire me daily. And to all creators and writers, who have kept me company through my life".

Introduction

Learning a language is not a simple task. It's challenging, and perfecting it can take a lifetime. During his First Inaugural Address on the 4th of March 1933, Franklin D. Roosevelt, the 32nd President of the US, claimed that "Happiness lies in the <u>joy</u> of <u>achievement</u> and the <u>thrill</u> of creative <u>effort</u>". Along with many philosophers and thinkers throughout history, I firmly believe that there's nothing more valuable in life than the accomplishments earned through sustained effort. Learning a second language and unlocking all its secrets is one of those valuable things in life.

Fully immersed in the era of technology, learning a foreign language without effort is still not possible. I often think of language learning as a long-distance trek up a mountain we have never explored before, marked by ever-changing terrains that demand adaptability. Yet, it also offers breathtaking views and a chance to appreciate rare plants and natural wonders we had never seen— landscapes not everyone can contemplate.

This exclusivity is akin to those who move beyond knowing just one language, to those who venture out from the insularity of their comfort zones and explore new lands. They don't merely learn a new language; they open themselves to wider horizons, deeper cultural insights, and a richer understanding of the world with new perspectives and ways of thinking.

Language shapes how we think, and the way we think changes our reality and our understanding of it. There are expressions in Spanish that we would never use in English, and vice versa. Learning a new language is opening the doors to a new culture, to a new way of thinking, to doing things in new ways. Can you imagine a world where you don't say "thank you" or "sorry" as often as we do in English? In India, it's more common to express gratitude through gestures or actions, but people don't use the word "thank you" as frequently. It's considered overly formal. This means that "thank you" has a totally different meaning in India and when translating the expression we don't fully capture its meaning in its cultural context because that word is not used in the same way we use it in English. We can only understand a different culture if we know its language and how it is used.

These are the lessons we learn through our language learning journey. When you approach the mountain's peak, not only do your horizons broaden, but you also carry within the profound wisdom of your ascent.

In a practical and specific manner, I hope this book advances your journey to the summit or helps in bridging the gaps you weren't aware existed—those little mistakes nobody ever explained to you. I trust you'll also take moments to pause, rest, and appreciate the exquisite nature-inspired illustrations on this linguistic ascent, drawing you nearer to the pinnacle of Spanish mastery.

From inspiration to creation

I recall a particular day from my childhood when I read that J.K. Rowling conceived the world of Harry Potter on a train journey. Quite impressive! I remember thinking, "Will I ever write a book myself?" My passion for books was profound back then, and I often daydreamed about becoming a writer one day. It wasn't just the narratives that captivated me; I was equally drawn to any kind of book. I liked them as objects, exquisite objects. My grandmother had hundreds of them and, to me, they were like small works of art, with their diverse shapes, colours, fonts, covers, and interior designs.

Years later, being already a teacher, I observed how my students used to make the same similar mistakes in Spanish. Over time, I began compiling a list of these common errors along with explanations, serving as quick references to aid my pupils. I would distribute these lists and encourage students to reflect about why their sentences were not correct, followed by providing them with answers and brief activities to practise, helping them avoid such mistakes.

One Christmas, when I returned to my mother's house, I isolated myself in the home library. While browsing through the books, I stumbled upon an old book that had greatly helped me to improve my English during my time as a student at the University of Sheffield. It was a simple short book featuring a collection of erroneous English sentences alongside explanations. That book significantly contributed to refining my English skills and deepening my understanding of the language mechanisms. It illuminated those intricate aspects of language that one never fully comprehends—details that can genuinely elevate your proficiency.

Upon my return to England, I embarked on creating this book which took me 2 years. The edition of the book took me 3 months. I did not want the book to be a boring dull-looking dictionary, workbook or grammar book with a Spanish flag on the cover and bulls and paellas illustrations through the book. I wanted the book to be beautiful and have its own "personality".

I hope it proves as invaluable to you as it has to my students and, in a similar vein, as its English counterpart was to me. In this book you will find the 80 most common mistakes that English native speakers make in Spanish, along with explanations on how to avoid them and activities (with answers) to practise.

One of the aspects I relished most about learning English and French was the boundless realm of new books that language acquisition opened up to me. The journey of learning languages is truly enchanting, and I hope it unlocks doors to wondrous new worlds for you to explore as it did to me.

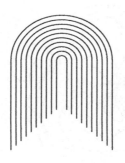

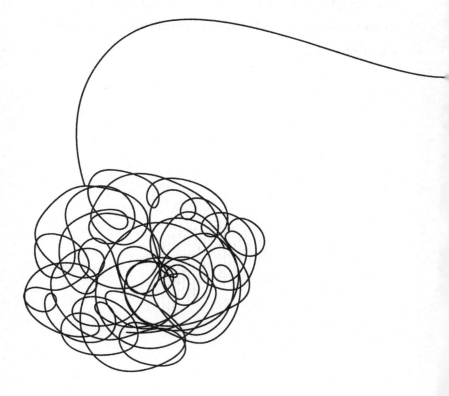

The 80 Most Common Mistakes in Spanish

How to use this book?

This book is aimed at those who have a mid level in Spanish but even if your level is medium-high there is more than one thing to take away. A Spanish native speaker or someone with an advanced level of Spanish would know, upon reading the list of mistakes, that they are mistakes. Feel free to use this book as you like. You can read it in a linear way or explore by choosing mistakes that catch your attention. Perhaps you'll read a sentence in the list of mistakes and notice that you don't know why it's wrong. Then, you can go to the explanation, read it and you'll gain new insights.

The mistakes all have the same structure and look like this:

0. Mistake in Spanish // English original sentence

✗ English original sentence = <u>Mistaken</u> translation in Spanish.

✓ English original sentence= <u>Correct</u> sentence in Spanish.

You can jump through the book. You will also find an activities section. There, I've condensed several common mistakes from the book into these exercises. In just one activity 3-4 mistakes can be involved. I kindly recommend giving these activities a go after you've used the book a few times or when you feel prepared. I've strived to ensure consistency in presenting the same mistakes in different ways within the activities. This approach will help solidify your learning and ensure its endurance.

Lastly, at the book's end, you'll discover the answers accompanied by brief explanations.

THE 80 MOST COMMON MISTAKES IN SPANISH

1. Es bien

2. Soy en el colegio

3. Soy jugando al ordenador

4. Soy aburrido

5. Soy cansado

6. Soy un poco corto pero mi hermano es alto

7. Soy frío

8. Soy 25 años

9. Soy bueno al francés

10. Tengo azules ojos

11. Tengo rubio pelo

12. Tengo una grande casa

13. Inglaterra es cerca de Francia

14. Tú juegas al fútbol muy bien

15. Me gusta porque interesante

16. Actualmente no lo sé

17. Es la más interesante asignatura

18. Es me asignatura preferida

19. Las matemáticas es bien

20. Estoy tarde

21. Voy a la librería

22. Mi padre está a París

23. Es bastante una interesante persona

24. Zak es mi hermano más viejo

25. La casa es muy anciana

26. Hay es 5 habitaciones en mi casa

27. Es muy calor

28. La problema es muy seria

29. Mi casa es tranquilo y pequeño

30. Mi casas son bonitas

31. Voy a juego al baloncesto

32. Voy a el parque

33. Llegó tarde porque de el autobús

34. Me jugar futbol

35. Me gusto correr porque es entretenido

36. Me gusta los perros porque son bonitos

37. Me prefiero comer la pizza

38. Me gusta café porque es sano

39. Estoy en amor con mi novio

40. Español es difícil, pero mucha gente lo habla

41. No me gusta el pescado, pero mi madre come lo

42. Los exámenes son dificils

43. La casa es bastante larga

44. En domingo normalmente juego al fútbol

45. ¿Puedo tener un café, por favor?

46. Me encanta mucho

47. ¿Qué es tu número de teléfono?

48. Tuve que preguntar por direcciones

49. Mi padre tiene no bigote

50. Me gustaría casarse con un chico guapo

51. Me llevo bien con mis abuelos porque es comprensivo

52. Ayer usé mi móvil ver vídeos

53. He escribido una carta a la Reina

54. Estoy mirando por mis llaves

55. La gente son muy amables

56. Este libro es mucho interesante

57. No problema

58. Tomé a mi hermana al aeropuerto

59. Me gustan acción películas

60. Mi madre siempre me soporta en mis decisiones

61. El chico vivo con es muy sucio

62. Te veo en la mañana

63. Soy un cocinero

64. Mi hermano está embarazado

65. Me duelen mis ojos

66. Hago muchos errores cuando hablo español

67. Voy a tomar un otro bocadillo

68. Esto no hace sentido

69. Estamos esperando por el autobús

70. Mi móvil no trabaja

71. Ayer tuve un montón de divertido en la fiesta

72. Fui a Francia tres tiempos el año pasado

73. El más aprendo el más me gusta

74. Mi madre quiere yo estudio 3 horas al día

75. Mi hermano llamó mi madre una idiota

76. Ten cuidado cuando viajando con lluvia fuerte

77. Puedo hablar con mis amigos quien viven muy lejos

78. Pareces guapa

79. Viví aquí para dos años

80. Si habría estudiado más, habría aprobado el examen

1. Es bien // It's good

✘   It's good = Es **bien**.

✓   It's good = Es **bueno**.

"Bien" (well) and "Bueno" (good) are commonly confused. "Bueno" is an adjective, which means it's used only to describe nouns. On the other hand, "Bien" is an adverb, used to describe how the action of a verb is performed.

For example, in the sentence "como bien" which translates to "I eat well", the adverb "bien" describes how I eat (well). Another example of an adverb would be "Como rápido" which means "I eat quickly" where "quickly", serves as an adverb to describe the way I eat (quickly). As you can see "rápido" describes the action of eating. Other examples are:

I played really well = Jugué realmente bien.

I can't swim well = No puedo nadar bien.

Unlike "bien," which remains the same, "bueno" changes to agree with the noun it describes because it is an adjective. For instance:

Mi casa es buena = My house is good.
El ordenador es bueno = The computer is good.

Las alfombr<u>as</u> son buen<u>as</u> = The rugs are good.

In English, saying "I am well" and "I am good" can often be used interchangeably and convey the same meaning. However, in Spanish, "Estoy bueno" and "Estoy bien" are entirely different. "Soy bueno" means "I am good," either as a good person or skilled at something (e.g., "Soy bueno al fútbol").

Conversely, "Estoy bueno" translates to "I am hot," referring to being attractive. The phrase "Soy bien" is not grammatically correct in Spanish. It would erroneously imply that your permanent state of being is good.

"Estoy bien" means "I am well" and conveys a sense of feeling good or being okay.

Similarly, to express that something is good, we use "es bueno". To clarify further:

Estoy bien = I am well.
Estoy bueno/a = I am hot.
Soy bueno = I'm good (as in I'm a good person).
Está bueno/a = It's tasty.
Es bueno = It's good.
Está bien = He/She/It is well or "It's ok".
No te preocupes, está bien = Do not worry, it's ok.

2. Soy en el colegio // I am at school

✗   I am at school = <u>Soy</u> en el colegio.

✓   I am at school = <u>Estoy</u> en el colegio.

The Spanish language has two verbs that translate to the English verb "to be": "ser" and "estar". This duality often confuses English speakers, as the English language uses just one verb to express "being". Misusing "ser" and "estar" is a common mistake among those learning Spanish. But fear not! Understanding the rules for their use is straightforward.

Both "ser" and "estar" mean "to be" and describe a state or condition. However, the key difference lies in the duration and permanency of that state. "Ser" is used to describe long-lasting, more permanent states or characteristics, while "estar" is used for temporary, changeable conditions.

For instance, if you want to say "I am sad" in Spanish, you would use "estar" because sadness is generally considered a temporary emotional state. So, "I am sad" translates to "Estoy triste". If you were to say "Soy triste," it would imply that you are fundamentally a sad person, suggesting a long-lasting condition. You might elaborate by saying, "Soy triste; es mi personalidad," which means "I am a sad person; it's my personality".

Location is another factor that usually entails change, especially when talking about a person's whereabouts. Therefore, "estar" is always used to describe locations. One could argue that while a person's location may change, a building's location is permanent. As always, grammar rules are not perfect! In this case, we need to remember that "estar" is always used for locations.

Other examples of conditions that are temporary include things like:

The TV is off = La tele <u>está</u> apagada.
The fridge is open = El frigo <u>está</u> abierto.

In fixed or long-term conditions, we include jobs:

My mum is a doctor = Mi madre <u>es</u> doctora.

Remember:

Use "ser" for long-term or fixed things, such as characteristics, personality, time, origin, and relationships.

Use "estar" for short-term or changing things like emotions, locations, and conditions.

3. Soy jugando al ordenador // I'm playing on my computer

✗ I'm playing on my computer = <u>Soy</u> jugando con mi ordenador.

✓ I'm playing on my computer = <u>Estoy</u> jugando con mi ordenador.

Sometimes it can be challenging to remember when to use "estoy" versus "soy" in Spanish. In the context of the present continuous tense, which in English is structured as "I am + verb-ing," the appropriate verb to use is always "estar". For example:

"I am singing" translates to "Estoy cantando".
"She is cooking" translates to "Está cocinando".

The same rule applies when using the past continuous tense, or any other continuous tenses: we must always use the past form of "estar" not "ser". Example:

She was coming = Estaba viniendo (not era viniendo).

4. Soy aburrido // I am bored

✗   I am bored = **Soy** aburrido.

✓   I am bored = **Estoy** aburrido.

As we have seen, we use the verb "ser" for long-lasting or permanent things whereas we use "estar" for short-term situations.

When we want to express that we are bored, it is normally a description of how we are feeling, and feelings are transitory and not permanent. Therefore, we would use "estar":

I am bored = Estoy aburrido.

When we say "Soy aburrido" that translates to "I am boring".

5. Soy cansado // I am tired

✗   I am tired = **Soy** cansado.

✓   I am tired = **Estoy** cansado.

This case is similar to the one mentioned above, but I want to emphasise a particular slang term in Spanish. When you want to say that you are tired, you would use "estoy" because tiredness is usually a temporary condition. If you were to say "soy cansado," it would imply something more like "I'm tiring" or "I am a pain" In this context, another term to describe someone as burdensome or annoying is "pesado," which literally means "heavy" but figuratively refers to being "a pain".

6. Soy un poco corto pero mi hermano es alto// I am a bit short, but my brother is tall.

✗ I am a bit short, but my brother is tall = Soy un poco **corto** pero mi hermano es alto.

✓ I am a bit short, but my brother is tall = Soy un poco **bajo** pero mi hermano es alto.

In English, we would use the word "short" both to describe hair length and height. In Spanish, when describing short height, we use "bajo" whilst we use "corto" to describe short hair.

7. Soy frío // I am cold

✗ I am cold = **Soy** frío.

✓ I am cold = **Tengo** frío.

If you have read mistake 1, you will know that "soy frío" implies a sort of long-term description, suggesting that you are a cold person by nature. To express that you are feeling cold at the moment, you would say "tengo frío", as if you had the cold inside your bones.

Another similar mistake occurs when we want to say "I have a cold". It would not be literally translated as "tengo un frío", but rather "tengo un resfriado" or "estoy resfriado". Again, we use "estoy" because it is a transient state, not a fixed one.

8. Soy 25 años // I am 25 years old

✗   I am 25 years old = <u>Soy</u> 25 años.

✓   I am 25 years old = **<u>Tengo</u>** 25 años.

This is one of the most common mistakes. It tends to happen when translating literally and forgetting that sometimes languages don't work in the same way.

In Spanish, we say that people "<u>have</u> years" not how old they <u>are</u>. When we say in Spanish "Tengo 25 años" that literally means "I have 25 years". Think of it as if possessing the years in the form of wisdom or experience.

Understanding this concept can be challenging, but the explanation lies in the fact that languages operate differently. In other languages like French or Italian, indicating your age follows the same pattern as in

Spanish: "J'ai 25 ans" (I have 25 years) and "Ho 25 anni" (I have 25 years), respectively. Greek uses the verb "to be" instead of "to have," so they would say "είμαι 25 χρονών" (I am of 25 years). In Chinese, a verb is not even used, and people simply state "我25岁" (I 25 years). German shares a similarity with English: "Ich bin 25" (I am 25).

9. Soy bueno al francés // I am good at French

✗   I am good at French = Soy bueno **al** francés.

✓   I am good at French = Soy bueno **en** francés.

As mentioned before, when translating the English word "good" into Spanish, we must use the word "bueno/a".. "Bien" means "well".

In Spanish, when discussing proficiency or skill in a specific sport, we use the construction "bueno al" followed by the name of the sport. For example, "bueno al hockey" means "good at hockey," and "bueno al baloncesto" means "good at basketball". This construction emphasizes expertise or ability in that particular sport.

On the other hand, when referring to being good or proficient in a broader sense, not limited to a specific sport, we use the construction "bueno en" followed by the subject. For instance, "bueno en matemáticas" translates to "good at maths," and "bueno en baile" means "good at dancing". This construction is more general and can be applied to various skills or talents. We would not say "Bueno al matemáticas", but "Bueno en matemáticas".

It's important to note that while "bueno al" is specific to sports, "bueno en" can be used to describe proficiency or competence in any subject, activity, or sport. Understanding these subtle differences in usage allows for more accurate and appropriate communication when expressing someone's skills or abilities in Spanish.

10. Tengo azules ojos // I have blue eyes

✖ I have blue eyes = Tengo azules ojos.

✓ I have blue eyes = Tengo **los** ojos azules.

This is a funny one because of how my young pupils react to it. When I teach them how to describe eyes, I always say that Spanish word order is awkward, and I teach them the sentence "I have THE eyes blues" so that they can remember the word order in Spanish. I really emphasize THE, and they always laugh because of how exaggeratedly and loudly I say it. I use all the space on the board to write a huge THE.

I have <u>THE</u> eyes blues = Tengo <u>LOS</u> ojos azules.

This example helps them remember that word order is different in Spanish sometimes. Then I ask them: "Next time you're with your mum, point at someone and say: Look, mum, she has THE eyes blue! and tell me what she says next lesson!"

Then, the day after: "Sir, my mum asked me if I was ok!"

11. Tengo rubio pelo // I have blonde hair

✗   I have blonde hair = Tengo rubio pelo.

✓   I have blonde hair= Tengo **el pelo rubio**.

Very similar to mistake 10, word order in Spanish is different! We also need THE and, if you look carefully, the adjective describing hair needs to agree with the noun, so in this case if you had blonde hair we would not say "Tengo el pelo rubio<u>s</u>", but "Tengo el pelo rubio", as pelo is masculine and singular (ojos is plural, therefore azul<u>es</u>).

Tengo el pelo castaño = I have brown hair.

12. Tengo una grande casa // I have a big house

✗   I have a big house = Tengo una **grande** casa.

✓   I have a big house = Tengo una casa **grande**.

We normally put the adjective after the noun in Spanish, and I say normally because there are some exceptions. For instance, when we say "She is my best friend", we would say "Es mi mejor amiga". Whenever we say that something is the best, we place the adjective before the noun.

Also, sometimes we put it before like in:

My aunt is a good person = Mi tía es una buena persona.

However, it would also work if we said "Mi tía es una persona buena" although with a touch of Yoda-style phrasing, exuding an air of wisdom upon altering the word order.

Interestingly, in some cases, the position of the adjective can change the meaning completely, like when we say:

Es un hombre pobre = He is a poor man (lacking money).
Es un pobre hombre = He is a poor man (pitiable, unfortunate).

In most cases, the adjective goes after the noun, like in the example above where we would need to say "casa grande" as we would say "mesa azul" or "coche rápido".

13. Inglaterra es cerca de Francia // England is close to France

✗ England is close to France = Inglaterra <u>es</u> cerca de Francia.

✓ England is close to France = Inglaterra <u>está</u> cerca de Francia.

As pointed out in mistake 2, when we are talking about location, we use "estar". Also, note that we say "cerca de". This is called *colocation*. Like in English, certain prepositions go with some particles. For example, we normally say "think + about" or "think + of" but it's not grammatically correct to say "I'm thinking <u>in</u> you". In Spanish "close to" translates into "cerca de" which literally means "close of".

14. Tú juegas al fútbol muy bien // You play football very well

✗   You play football very well = <u>**Tú**</u> juegas al fútbol muy bien.

✓   You play football very well = Juegas al fútbol muy bien.

This sentence is not technically wrong. However, native speakers omit pronouns in most cases due to the nature of the language. We don't need to say "tú juegas" as the ending of jue<u>gas</u> already indicates that <u>you</u> are playing.

Pronouns are used to clarify who is performing the action if it's not clear, or to emphasise our message.

15. Me gusta porque interesante // I like it because it is interesting

✗   I like it because it is interesting = Me gusta porque interesante.

✓   I like it because it is interesting = Me gusta porque <u>**es**</u> interesante.

Forgetting to include the verb in a sentence occurs quite frequently. This can be attributed to how our brains process language and communication.

Let's consider "Harry más alto que Ana" (Harry taller than Ana) instead of "Harry **es** más alto que Ana" (Harry **is** taller than Ana). If we think about it, when comparing Harry's height to Ana's, we don't really need to use the verb "is" to convey that Harry is taller than Ana. We read "Harry taller than Ana" and we perfectly get the whole message. The word "is" is superfluous here for the message to be conveyed. The reason why we sometimes forget it in Spanish is because it is not necessary to communicate the message and therefore our brain automatically omits something that we don't need.

This phenomenon of omitting the verb when it is not necessary is so deeply ingrained in our brain's natural language processing that it is part of many languages and it has been given a name: *zero copula*, which means that the subject of the sentence is connected to the predicate <u>without</u> a verb. Although we don't use it in English an example could be "I don't like them because they stupid," where "they" is the subject and "stupid" is the predicate.

This phenomenon of *zero copula* is present in several languages including Bengali, Chinese, Indonesian, Turkish, Hindi, Turkmen, Japanese, Ukrainian, Hungarian, Hebrew, Arabic, Hawaiian, Irish, Welsh, Lithuanian, Latvian, Polish, Slovakian, and Quechua.

However, even though our brains naturally tend to simplify the message by omitting the verb, it is important to note that in Spanish, we should not use *the zero copula*. In other words, we should not forget to include the verb as doing so is not grammatically correct.

16. Actualmente no lo sé // Actually, I don't know

✗   Actually, I don't know = **Actualmente,** no lo sé.

✓   Actually, I don't know = **En realidad,** no lo sé.

"Actualmente" is a false friend in Spanish. It means "currently".

Actualmente estoy aprendiendo francés = Currently I'm learning French.

When we want to say "actually" we use different formulas in Spanish, like for example "en realidad" (in reality). An alternative is "realmente" (really) or we could say "de hecho" (in fact).

17. Es la más interesante asignatura // It's the most interesting subject

✖ It's the most interesting subject = Es la más interesante **asignatura**.

✓ It's the most interesting subject = Es la **asignatura** más interesante.

Word order again! *Ay señor!* We think in English and translate literally, and it turns out it's not the same in Spanish.

In this case, when we use "the most" and "the least", we have a special structure we can follow, called the <u>superlative</u>.

Lucky us, the superlative (and many other structures) works like things in maths, applying a formula:

English	Spanish
The + most/less + adjective + noun	The + noun + most/less + adjective

Therefore, we would say in Spanish "It's the subject most interesting" (Es la asignatura más interesante).

18. Es me asignatura preferida // It's my favourite subject

✗ It's my favourite subject = Es **me** asignatura preferida.

✓ It's my favourite subject = Es **mi** asignatura preferida.

You may recognize this as a common error, and it's important to distinguish between making a mistake knowingly and making one unknowingly. This error often falls into the latter category. Because the English word "me" sounds similar to the Spanish word "mi", it's easy to mix up the vowels.

Also, we must remember that my changes to match the noun (mi casa = my house, mi_s_ casas = my house_s_).

19. Las matemáticas es bien // Maths is good

✗ Maths is good = Las matemáticas **es bien**.

✓ Maths is good =Las matemáticas **son buenas**.

Translating "Maths is good" can involve *three* possible and common mistakes. One has to do with *ser/estar* and we have discussed this in mistakes 2, 4 and 5. The other one is related to mistake 1 (using "bueno/bien"). In this case, we would use "bueno" (good) like in English, but we have to make it agree with the noun "matemáticas" which is a feminine and plural word. Therefore, we would say: "Las matemátic<u>as</u> son buen<u>as</u>".

Also, because mathematics (matemáticas) is plural we would use "son" (are) not "es" (is).

Finally, as we can see in mistake 40, we are starting a sentence with a noun so we must add <u>THE</u> to the noun "maths".

20. Estoy tarde // I'm late

✖   I'm late = **<u>Estoy</u>** tarde.

✓   I'm late = **<u>Llego</u>** tarde.

In Spanish, you can't "be late". Is that not amazing? Perhaps, the language is a reflection of the culture! In Spanish, you say "Voy tarde" (I'm going late) or "Llegar/venir tarde" (to come/arrive late).

If we imagine some situations where someone is late this is what people would say in Spanish:

In a lesson where a student is late, the teacher would say:

Pedro, ¿por qué llegas tan tarde, qué ha pasado? (Pedro why are you so late, what happened?)

A friend who apologises for coming late:

"Lo siento por llegar tarde", "Disculpa que llegue tarde" or "Lo siento por venir tarde".

We would never say "soy tarde" or "estoy tarde".

21. Voy a la librería // I go to the library

✗   I go to the library = Voy a la **librería**.

✓   I go to the library = Voy a la **biblioteca**.

A *false friend* in the context of languages refers to a word that may sound or look similar in two languages but has different meanings. The word "librería" is a *false friend*. While "librería" may resemble the English word "library", it actually means "bookshop" in Spanish.

To clarify further, the word for "library" in Spanish is "biblioteca". Interestingly, "biblioteca" can be broken down into "biblio-" which relates to *bibles* and "-teca" which means a place or room. Therefore, "biblioteca" literally translates to "the bibles/books room".

In English, we have a related term called "bibliography". This term refers to a list of books or other sources used in research or academic work. The connection between "biblioteca" and "bibliography" can be seen in the shared root "biblio-", which both languages inherited from Greek, indicating a relationship with books.

So, it's important to note that although "librería" and "library" may sound similar, they have different meanings. This serves as an example of a false friend in language learning, highlighting the need for careful attention to avoid confusion when translating between languages.

Other common false friends include:

- Actual: In English, "actual" typically means "current" or "present," but in Spanish, "actual" means "real" or "genuine". For example, "El libro actual" means "The current book", not "The actual book".

- Embarazada: This false friend often catches English speakers off guard. While "embarazada" may look similar to "embarrassed," it actually means "pregnant" in Spanish. So, be cautious when using it and make sure to use "avergonzado/a" for "embarrassed".

- Sensible: In English, "sensible" typically means having good judgment or being reasonable. However, in Spanish, "sensible" means "sensitive" or "emotional". So, if you want to express "sensible" in the English sense, you would use "razonable" or "sensato" in Spanish.

- Carpeta: In Spanish, "carpeta" may seem like it refers to a carpet. However, in Spanish, "carpeta" means a "folder" or "file". So, when asking for a carpet in Spanish, use "alfombra" instead.

22. Mi padre está a París // My dad is in Paris

✗ My dad is in Paris = Mi padre está <u>a</u> París.

✓ My dad is in Paris = Mi padre está <u>en</u> París.

I often find that students who have studied French in primary school make this mistake. I remember my French teacher insisting "When we refer to a city we use "à" (à Paris, à Londres, Je suis à Paris). However, in Spanish, like in English, we use "in" (en). For instance:

Estoy en París, Estoy en Londres, Estoy en Nueva York.

It doesn't matter if we are in a country; we say "Estoy en Francia". Neither does it matter if we're indicating location somewhere else like on the train, on the beach, in the swimming pool, or at school. We always use the preposition en.

I am <u>on</u> the beach = Estoy <u>en</u> la playa.
I am <u>on</u> the train = Estoy <u>en</u> el tren.
I am <u>in</u> the swimming pool = Estoy <u>en</u> la piscina.
I am <u>at</u> the school = Estoy <u>en</u> la escuela.

The only time we use "a" is when we say that we go <u>to</u> a place. "Voy <u>a</u> Francia" = "I go <u>to</u> France". Another common mistake I often see is: "Voy de vacaciones <u>en</u> Francia", where they actually mean "I go on holidays <u>TO</u> France" (Voy de vacaciones <u>a</u> Francia).

23. Es bastante una interesante persona // She is quite an interesting person

✗   She is quite an interesting person = Es **<u>bastante una interesante persona</u>**.

✓   She is quite an interesting person = Es **<u>una persona bastante interesante</u>**.

When we have this kind of grammatical construction:

1. Pronoun + Verb + Intensifier* + Article + Adjective + Noun
2. Pronoun + Verb + Article + Intensifier* + Adjective + Noun

It corresponds to the following Spanish grammatical construction:

3. Verb + Article + Noun + Intensifier* + Adjective

Then if we have something like in number 1 "This is quite an old house" that would correlate to the formula as follows:

This	is	quite	an	old	house
Pronoun	Verb	Intensifier	Article	Adjective	Noun

The article can go before the intensifier as well, as when we say "This is a very old house" that would correlate to the second formula as follows:

This	is	a	very	old	house
Pronoun	Verb	Article	Intensifier	Adjective	Noun

In Spanish, we normally omit the pronoun, so the sentence begins with is/are:

Es	una	casa	bastante/muy	vieja
Verb	Article	Noun	Intensifier	Adjective

If you find this grammar too complicated to remember, as it was for me, something that helps is to change the word order in English to mimic the Spanish word order. This way is easier to remember it.

Therefore, we change the word order in English, so it matches the word order in Spanish:

3. Verb + Article + Noun + Intensifier* + Adjective

Examples:

This is quite an old house -> This is a house quite old.

She is quite an interesting person -> She is a person quite interesting.

They are a very good couple -> They are a couple very good.

She is a bit of a weird person sometimes -> She is a person a bit weird sometimes.

Then we can translate word for word:

This is a house quite old = Es una casa bastante vieja.
She is a person quite interesting = Es una persona bastante interesante.
They are a couple very good = Son una pareja muy buena.
She is a person a bit weird sometimes= Es una persona un poco rara a veces.

*Intensifiers are words that change the intensity of adjectives like (a little, very, quite). He is quite shy tells you how shy (adjective) he is.

24. Zak es mi hermano más viejo // Zak is my older brother

✗ Zak is my older brother = Zak es mi hermano más <u>viejo</u>.

✓ Zak is my older brother = Zak es mi hermano <u>mayor</u>.

While people would understand what you're trying to say if you use the phrase "mi hermano más viejo," the terms "viejo," "mayor," "menor," and "pequeño" work differently in Spanish than in English when discussing age. For example, "older brother" translates to "hermano mayor," not "hermano más viejo". Similarly, "younger brother" is "hermano menor," not a literal translation of "hermano más joven".

In Spanish, we express age differently than in English; we describe how many years someone "has" rather than how "old" they are. Therefore, the terms "viejo" and "joven" are not used in the same way as in English when discussing age.

To summarize, while you can use "joven" and "viejo" to indicate that someone is young or old (e.g., "mi hermano es muy viejo"), it's important to use "mayor" and "menor" when specifically referring to older or younger siblings.

25. La casa es muy anciana // The house is very old

✘   The house is very old = La casa es muy **anciana**.

✓   The house is very old = La casa es muy **vieja**.

"Anciano" reminds us of "ancient" in English, something belonging to the very distant past and no longer in existence, that is...very old! In English, the word comes from the old French word "ancient" which, in turn, comes from the Latin word "ante" meaning before. When words come from Latin they sometimes evolve differently and mean different things in different languages. For example, the modern French word "ancient" means "very old" but also "former", like when we say "the former president" (L'ancien president). However, "anciano" in Spanish doesn't have that meaning. We say "El antiguo presidente" or "El presidente anterior" (the former president).

The word "<u>antiguo</u>" means "old" but also "former" in Spanish. When used as old, it is used like "antique" in English for objects like cars, furniture, buildings, etc.

Examples:

Estas casas son muy <u>antiguas</u> = These houses are very old.
Este coche es muy <u>antiguo</u> = This car is very old.

Esta ciudad es muy <u>antigua</u> = This city is very old.

When we use it with people, it indicates their former post, occupation, etc. Example:

Juan es el <u>antiguo</u> director de la escuela = Juan is the former school headteacher.

Finally, we can say that someone is "antiguo" and it means they're old-fashioned in their way of thinking/behaving. However, this doesn't imply that they are old necessarily. Example:

Pedro es muy antiguo, ya nadie piensa así = Pedro is very old-fashioned, nobody thinks like that anymore.

On the other hand, we have "<u>anciano</u>", which is used only to express that someone is very old. Let's summarise:

1. "<u>Anciano</u>" means very old, and it is only used for people: "El presidente es un anciano" (The president is a very old person).

2. "<u>Antiguo</u>" means "former" and "antique". We use it for people when we say "former" and for objects in all other cases.

3. "<u>Viejo</u>" is our go-to word when we want to say old. It works with objects and people.

Finally, a funny anecdote about language learning. Once upon a time, when I was a student, I was living with a family in France to improve my French. We were having dinner and a friend of the family joined us that night.

He said something about being the former head teacher of a school, but I wasn't sure. In a flashback, I remembered that lesson when my teacher explained to us: "Be careful, there are two words in French: "ancient" and "antique". One means "former", the other means "antique". Be careful not get them mixed up!". I couldn't remember which one was which, so I asked him "Excusez-moi, avez-vous dit que vous étiez l'antique directeur d'ecole?" Everyone at the table was laughing. I called the respectable gentleman an antique!

Being laughed at is part of learning a language! At least we make people happy through our language-learning journey.

26. Hay es 5 habitaciones en mi casa // There are 5 rooms in my house

✗ There are 5 rooms in my house = Hay **es** 5 habitaciones en mi casa.

✓ There are 5 rooms in my house = Hay 5 habitaciones en mi casa.

Because in English we have two words for "there is" or "there are" we tend to think that we need two in Spanish. Therefore, people think "There = hay" and "is = es". However, we need to remember that "hay" comes from the infinitive form of the verb "haber". In this way, "haber" has different conjugations depending on the tense:

There will be = Habrá
There is = Hay
There was = Había
There would be = Habría

Therefore, we don't have to add "es" as it does not correspond to the English "is" when used in the "there is/are" construction. It's a different construction and the word "hay" means "there is" or "there are" as the word "habrá" on its own means "there will be".

27. Es muy calor // It's very hot

✗   It's very hot = <u>Es</u> muy calor

✓   It's very hot = <u>Hace</u> mucho calor.

Ay madre mía, el tiempo! There are several variants to this error. I have seen "es mucho calor", "es muy caliente", or "es mucho caliente".

"Es muy caliente" means "it's very hot" but we use it when describing a very hot object, never for the weather. When we want to describe the weather today as hot we say "hace mucho calor". If we are describing a place like "Spain is very hot" we would say "En España hace mucho calor".

When we say "hace calor" in Spanish, it literally translates to "it makes heat". This may give the impression that the weather itself is being created by an entity like something is making it hot. However, it's important to understand that this is a linguistic construction rather than a literal description of weather creation.

If we consider the English language, we can find similar patterns. For example, we say "it's windy" , using an adjective to describe that the weather is windy. However, in a different way, we use the expressions "it rains" or "it's raining" to describe the action of rain falling, even though there is no specific subject identified in the sentence.

The use of "it" in these weather expressions serves as a grammatical placeholder or impersonal pronoun. It allows us to discuss weather conditions without attributing them to a particular entity. So, when we say "it rains," there is no specific "who" or "what" that is doing the action of raining. It is simply a way to acknowledge the weather phenomenon without assigning agency to a particular subject. This is used in a very similar way in Spanish and English.

The verb "llover" (to rain) is normally used in the 3rd person (llueve), and you will never see anything like "lluevo" (I rain). However, depending on the weather described, sometimes, that linguistic construction might use a different verb like "to make" (hacer). This is just a convention. These are some examples:

Hace sol = It's sunny.
Hace frío = It's cold.
Hace viento = It's windy.
Llueve = It rains.
Nieva = It snows.
Hay tormenta = There is a storm.
Está humedo = It's humid.

28. La problema es muy seria // The problem is very serious

✗ The problem is very serious = <u>La</u> problema es muy <u>seria</u>

✓ The problem is very serious = <u>El</u> problema es muy <u>serio</u>.

We know that in Spanish most adjectives must match the gender of the noun they describe. Therefore, if we want to say "a small house", the adjective "small" must match the gender of the word "house" (remember we switch the noun and adjective around and say a "house big"). We would then say:

A small house -> A house small = Una casa pequeña.

In Spanish, the adjective "small" can be translated to "pequeño, pequeña, pequeños, pequeñas" depending on the noun described. This rule applies to all adjectives that end with "-o" (masculine) or "-a" (feminine).

Those ending with "-e" like "grande" (big), "inteligente" (intelligent), or with consonants, like "fácil" (easy) or "difícil" (difficult) only become plural if the noun is plural, but the gender of this adjectives doesn't change.

The big <u>boy</u> = el <u>chico</u> grande.

The big **girls** = Las **chicas** grandes.

Going back to our mistake, the word "problema" might initially lead us to think that it's a feminine word because it ends with "-a". Generally, words ending with "-o" are masculine and words ending with "-a" are feminine.

However, there are exceptions to this rule. For example, "la mano" (the hand), "la foto" (the photo), "la disco" (the discotheque), "la moto" (the moped), and "la radio" (the radio) are all exceptions to the rule, as they end with "-o" but are feminine nouns. In addition to words ending with "-a", we need to remember that words ending with "**-ción**", "**-sión**", "**-dad**", "**-tad**", and "**-umbre**" are also feminine. For example, "la maldi_ción_" (the curse), "la deci_sión_" (the decision), "la ciu_dad_" (the city), "la mi_tad_" (the half), and "la c_umbre_" (the summit/peak) are all feminine.

Likewise, there are exceptions for words ending with "a" which can be masculine such as "el día" (the day), "el mapa" (the map), and "el sofá" (the sofa) which are all masculine. Nouns of Greek origin ending with "**-ma**" or "**-ta**" are also masculine, as in "el proble_ma_" (the problem), "el dra_ma_" (the drama), "el plane_ta_" (the planet), and "el profe_ta_" (the prophet).

Interestingly, in Spanish, some animals like "la hormiga" (the ant) or "la rana" (the frog) are referred to as feminine animals. When we want to specify their sex, we use "la hormiga macho" (the male ant) or "la hormiga hembra" (the female ant). We always say "la hormiga," never "el hormigo". Other examples include "el búho" (the owl), "la serpiente" (the snake), and "la paloma" (the pigeon) or "el águila" (the eagle).

Some other words use "el" or "la" depending on the gender of the person being referred to, such as "el estudiante" (the male student) or "la estudiante" (the female student). This is similar for "el/la testigo" (the male/female witness), "el/la violinista" (the male/female violinist), and "el/la mártir" (the male/female martyr).

Certain words have ambiguous genders, and "el" or "la" can be used interchangeably depending on the context or personal preference. Examples include "el/la calor" (the heat), "el/la azúcar" (the sugar), and "el/la mar" (the sea).

Finally, other exceptions include "el agua" (the wáter) which plural is "las aguas" when referring to the sea. We would also say "el alma" (the soul) but in plural would use "las almas" (the souls).

On top of this, there are other exceptions, like some colours. If you say for instance "the pink house" (la casa rosa) "rosa" matches "casa" but "rosa" won't change even if used to describe a masculine noun like "el vestido rosa" (the pink dress). Other colours like "rojo" (red) change depending on the noun they describe:

The red house = La casa roja.
The red cars = Los coches rojos.

29. Mi casa es tranquilo y pequeño // My house is quiet and small

✗   My house is quiet and small = Mi casa es **tranquila** y **pequeño**.

✓   My house is quiet and small = Mi casa es **tranquilo** y **pequeña**.

As explained above, "tranquilo" and "pequeño" are describing words, describing "casa". Therefore, the endings must agree with the noun being described (casa).

Sometimes learners struggle to identify what I call "the ruling word" which is the word dictating the endings of the other words in the sentence. The noun, the word being described by the adjectives, is the one deciding the endings of the adjectives. I ask my pupils to ask themselves the following when in doubt about a word ending:

1. Is it a describing word?
2. If so, what word is it describing?
3. Do the endings match?

30. Mi casas son bonitas // My houses are pretty

✘ My houses are pretty = <u>Mi</u> casas son bonitas.

✓ My houses are pretty = <u>Mis</u> casas son bonitas.

If we apply the previous mistake checklist and think about whether the word "my" is describing something about houses, the answer is yes (it is indicating that they "belong" to you). Therefore, "mi" is a describing word, it is and adjective and it must agree with "casas": Mi<u>s</u> casa<u>s</u>. "Mi" does not change for masculine and feminine.

31. Voy a juego al baloncesto // I'm going to play basketball

✗ I'm going to play basketball = Voy a **juego** al baloncesto.

✓ I'm going to play basketball = Voy a **jugar** al baloncesto.

This one drives me mad because it's the same structure as in English. "Voy a <u>juego</u> al baloncesto" is like saying in English "I am going <u>I play</u> basketball". The structure for this tense, the near future, is the same as in English: "Subject + verb to be + to go-ing + infinitive + complement". For some reason, we often forget that it's an infinitive and conjugate it as if it was in the first person of the present tense, with the -o ending.

"Voy a jueg<u>o</u> al baloncesto" means "I am going I play basketball".

"Voy a jug<u>ar</u> al baloncesto" means "I am going <u>to</u> play basketball".

32. Voy a el parque // I go to the park

✗   I go to the park = Voy <u>**a el**</u> parque.

✓   I go to the park = Voy <u>**al**</u> parque.

In Spanish, when we use the preposition "to" with a place, we have two options depending on whether the place is a masculine or feminine noun:

Masculine noun: A + el + place.
Feminine noun: A + la + place.

However, due to pronunciation reasons, the combination of "a" and "el" is contracted to "al" to sound smoother and more natural. So, instead of saying "Voy <u>a el</u> parque" (I'm going to the park), we say "Voy <u>al</u> parque".

This contraction doesn't happen with the feminine article "la". So we say: "Voy a la carnicería" (I'm going to the butcher's) without any change.

Similarly, when saying that we are coming from a place, we use the preposition "de" (from) followed by the article "el". However, we contract them to "del" for smoother pronunciation. For example, "Vengo <u>del</u> parque" (I'm coming from the park) instead of "Vengo <u>de el</u> parque".

It's important to note that this contraction only occurs with the singular masculine article "el," and it doesn't apply to <u>plural</u> forms of other articles in Spanish.

I'm going to the United States = Voy **a los** Estados Unidos.

33. Llegó tarde porque de el autobús // She arrived late because of the bus

✗ She arrived late because of the bus = Llegó tarde **porque de** el autobús.

✓ She arrived late because of the bus = Llegó tarde **por** el autobús.

The phrase "because of" is a connective that is commonly used to indicate causation or the reason behind something. An equivalent phrase is "due to". However, when translating this connective into Spanish, we cannot simply use a literal translation like "porque de" since that combination of words does not exist in Spanish.

Instead, when we want to use "because of" in Spanish, we need to use an appropriate equivalent preposition, such as "por" or "a causa de". For example, we would say "Llegó tarde por el autobús" to convey the meaning of "He/she arrived late because of the bus". If we choose to use "a causa de," we need to remember that when the preposition "de" is followed by the article "el," it contracts to "del". Therefore, we would say "Llegó tarde a causa del autobús" to mean the same thing.

It's important to note that the choice between "por" and "a causa de" depends on the context and personal preference. Both options are acceptable and convey the idea of causation or the reason behind something.

34. Me jugar futbol // I play football

✗   I play football = **Me jugar** al fútbol.

✓   I play football = **Juego** al fútbol.

The word "me" in Spanish is confusing. We tend to think that "me" in Spanish is equivalent to "me" in English, another word for "I". However, it works in a very different way. When we say "me" in Spanish we are indicating that the action in the sentence is directed to myself. This happens when we have a reflexive verb, meaning that the action is performed on yourself (like me ducho: I shower myself, me llamo: I call myself), but also in other cases.

One of those cases is when we say "me gusta el árbol". In Spanish, the concept of liking is different from English. In English, the subject likes someone or something. In Spanish, that someone or something causes a pleasant feeling in the subject, and therefore, the object is the one acting in the sentence while the subject receives that action.

Therefore, when you say in Spanish "me gusta el árbol" the tree is doing the action of pleasing me. That's why the ending is "-a" (gust__a__), which corresponds to the 3rd person, rather than "-o" which corresponds to the first person (I). It's not me doing the action but receiving it. It's the tree (it) performing the action of pleasing me. What "me gusta el árbol literally means then is "the tree pleases me" but it's translated into "I like the tree" as it is what we say in English. This is an interesting example of how different languages work in different ways.

When we say "me hablo" that means "I talk to myself". Therefore, "me" indicates that the action of the verb in that sentence is directed to me. If we just said "hablo" that would mean "I talk".

Similarly, when we use "te", it means that the action is performed on you. __Te__ hablo (I talk __to you__). __Te__ gusta (It pleases __you__/__You__ like it). __Se__ habla (He/she speaks __to himself/herself__).

English speakers, due to the similarity in the spellings of the word "me", tend to think that when we say "me gustan los árboles" in Spanish that means something like "me like trees" and therefore sometimes misuse the word. Examples of this include:

"Me jugar futbol" when they mean "juego al fútbol".
"Me comer pollo" when they mean "como pollo".

35. Me gusto correr porque es entretenido // I like to run because because it's entertaining

✗ I like to run because it's entertaining = Me **gusto** correr porque es entretenido.

✓ I like to run because it's entertaining = Me **gusta** correr porque es entretenido.

Building on the previous point, students sometimes assume that since the phrase "I like" uses the first person in English, the corresponding verb in Spanish should also end in "-o". However, the verb "gustar" functions differently, as explained in mistake 34. Saying "me gusto" actually means "I like myself," not "I like" in a general sense.

36. Me gusta los perros porque son bonitos // I like dogs because they are beautiful

✗ I like dogs because they are beautiful = Me **gusta** los perros porque son bonitos.

✓ I like dogs because they are beautiful = Me **gustan** los perros porque son bonitos.

I'd recommend reading first mistake 34 to better understand this one. When we use "me gusta" and the thing you like is a plural noun, you need to add "n" to "gusta". For example, "Me gusta la flor" (I like the flower) becomes "Me gustan las flores" (I like the flowers). It's the same with "me encanta". "Me encanta el pollo" (I love chicken) becomes "Me encantan los pollos" (I love chickens).

As briefly outlined in mistake 34, the use of "me" in "me gusta" indicates that the action is directed towards the speaker, as in it pleases the speaker (please see mistake 34 if you have any questions about what "me" means in Spanish and how to use it).

When we use "me gustan," it means that the plural object or objects please the subject. Note that the ending "-an" corresponds to the ending for "they" in the present tense.

The reason why the verb ending is "-a" or "-an" is because the object or objects are performing the action (<u>it</u> or <u>**they**</u> please).

Me gusta el arbol = The tree pleases me (literally "I like the tree").
Me gustan los árboles = The trees please me (literally "I like trees").

Present tense endings for AR verbs	
I	-o
You	-as
He/She/<u>**It**</u>	**-a**
We	-amos
You all	-áis
<u>**They**</u>	**-an**

The ending of "gustar" indicates who is doing the action of pleasing, therefore who or what we like. If we use a different ending like "me gus<u>tas</u>", then it would mean "<u>you</u> please me" (I like <u>you</u>) as we have used the ending for "you". It would be translated into "I like you" in English.

Equally, if someone who is not me likes something "me" would change.

Changes for gustar	
I like	Me
You like	Te
He/She/It likes	Le
We like	Nos
You all like	Os
They like	Les

You like trees = <u>Te</u> gustan los árboles.

She likes that tree = <u>Le</u> gusta ese árbol.

You like me = Te gusto.

You like yourself = Te gustas.

37. Me prefiero comer la pizza // I prefer to eat pizza

✖ I prefer to eat pizza = <u>Me</u> prefiero comer la pizza.

✓ I prefer to eat pizza = Prefiero comer la pizza.

A downside of Spanish is that we must learn by memory which verbs are reflexive. Whenever we have an infinitive which ends with "se", like "casar<u>se</u>" (to get married), we have a reflexive verb. Therefore, we are going to use "me" in the first person: "me caso hoy" (I get married today).

Sometimes we don't know whether a verb is reflexive or not and we put "me" with it. Preferir (to prefer) is not a reflexive verb and "me prefiero" is a common mistake as it is "me odio". If we say "me prefiero" that would mean "I prefer myself". "Me odio" means "I hate myself".

Me prefiero porque soy mi primera prioridad = I prefer myself because I am my first priority.

38. Me gusta café porque es sano // I like coffee because it's healthy

✗ I like coffee because it's healthy = Me gusta café porque es sano.

✓ I like coffee because it's healthy = Me gusta **el** café porque es sano.

This is one of the mistakes I see the most. The good news is that there is an easy way to avoid it! Whenever we use an opinion expression like "me gusta" (I like), "odio" (I hate), or "me encanta" (I love), we must include the definite article "**the**" before the thing we like/love/dislike/hate.

This rule applies when expressing our preferences or opinions. For example, instead of saying "I like coffee," in Spanish we say "I like THE coffee". The word "the" must agree with the noun it goes with.

Here are some examples to illustrate this rule:

I like maths = Prefiero <u>las</u> matemáticas.

I like science = Me gusta <u>la</u> ciencia.

I hate tea = Odio <u>el</u> té.

I'm interested in coffee = Me interesa <u>el</u> café (literally, "Coffee interests me".).

I'm fascinated by music = Me fascina <u>la</u> música (literally, "Music fascinates me.").

I prefer maths because it's challenging = Prefiero <u>las</u> matememáticas porque es un reto.

39. Estoy en amor con mi novio // I'm in love with my boyfriend

✗   I'm in love with my boyfriend = Estoy **en amor** con mi novio.

✓   I'm in love with my boyfriend = Estoy **enamorado de** mi novio.

In Spanish, "enamorarse" is a reflexive verb, like "casarse".

We need to distinguish carefully between "me encanta" and "me enamora", or "estoy enamorado de". If you say to someone "me encantas" they can understand it as you like them very much, or you love them. It is somehow used in different contexts. You can say "Me encanta Juan, es muy gracioso" (I love Juan, he is very funny). When we say "Estoy enamorado de Juan", that means, unequivocally, that you are romantically in love with him, and you have feelings for him.

40. Español es difícil, pero mucha gente lo habla // Spanish is difficult, but many people speak it

✗ Spanish is difficult but many people speak it
Español es difícil pero mucha gente lo habla.

✓ Spanish is difficult but many people speak it
<u>El</u> español es difícil pero mucha gente lo habla.

In Spanish, a grammatical rule states that whenever we begin a sentence with a noun, we must include the definite article "the" before it.

Here are some examples to illustrate this rule:
Tea is good for your health = <u>El</u> té es bueno para tu salud.
Spanish is easy = <u>El</u> español es fácil.
Languages are useful = <u>Los</u> lenguajes son útiles.

Similarly, when we start a sentence with a connective or conjunction + noun, such as "however" (sin embargo), "on the one hand" (por un lado), or "I think that" (pienso que), we must also include "the" before the noun.

However, tea is good = Sin embargo, <u>el</u> té es bueno.
I think that Spanish is easy = Pienso que <u>el</u> español es fácil.
On the other hand, languages are useful = Por otro lado, <u>los</u> lenguajes son útiles.

41. No me gusta el pescado, pero mi madre come lo // I don't like fish, but my mum eats it

✗ I don't like fish but my mum eats it = No me gusta el pescado, pero mi madre **come lo**.

✓ I don't like fish but my mum eats it = No me gusta el pescado, pero mi madre **lo come**.

In English, "it" can be the subject of a sentence performing an action or an object, receiving it. For instance:

"It" as a **subject**: <u>This plane</u> can fly, yes, <u>it</u> can fly.
"It" as an **object**: I eat <u>fish</u>, yes, I eat <u>it</u>.

In Spanish, when we use the pronoun "it" (lo) in a sentence and it's acting as an <u>object</u> (therefore receiving the action) it is placed before the verb. In English that "it" is placed after the verb, so we need to switch it around like this:

I never eat <u>fish</u>, no, I never eat <u>it</u>. -> I never eat fish, no, I never <u>it</u> eat. -> Nunca como <u>pescado</u>, no, nunca <u>lo</u> como.

Let's see other examples:

I see <u>it</u> = <u>Lo</u> veo
Don't say that! Don't say <u>it</u>! = No digas eso! ¡No <u>lo</u> digas!
I can't believe <u>it</u> = No <u>lo</u> puedo creer.

I saw it = Lo vi.

However, when there is more than one verb in the sentence and "it" is used with some verbs like "me gusta", "poder", "querer", "saber", "deber", "prefiero", etc, the position changes and "it" blends together with the second verb.

Let's see some examples:

I like to see it = Me gusta verlo (We would never say "Me gusta lo ver").

I can say it = Puedo decirlo.
I should believe it = Debo creerlo.
I can see it = Puedo verlo.
I know how to say it = Sé cómo decirlo.
I prefer to see it = Prefiero verlo.

Finally, note that "lo" can also refer to him and "la" to her.
I saw him in the pool = Lo vi en la piscina
I saw her in the pool = La vi en la piscina.
I will hug him if I see him = Lo abrazaré si lo veo

42. Los exámenes son dificils // Exams are difficult

✘   Exams are difficult = Los exámenes son **dificils**

✓   Exams are difficult = Los exámenes son **difíciles**.

In Spanish, we can form the plural of most words by adding "-s" to the singular form. Let's look at some examples:

"Manzana" (apple) becomes "Manzanas" (apples).
"Cosa" (thing) becomes "Cosas" (things).
"Blanco" (white) becomes "Blancos" (white).

However, this only applies to words ending in a vowel. It's slightly different to words ending with a constant or a z.

When a word ends in a consonant (any letter that is not a vowel: a, e, i, or u), such as "difícil" (difficult) or "fácil" (easy), we add "-es" to make it plural. Examples: difíciles (difficult), fáciles (easy).

If a word ends with "-z" and we want to make it plural, we replace "-z" with "-ces". Example: Feliz (happy) becomes Felices (happy). Remember the phrase "Feliz Navidad" meaning "Merry Christmas".

To illustrate these rules, let's consider the following example:

If we wanted to say "my parents are happy," we would say "Mis padres son feli<u>ces</u>". In this case, the word "felices" is the plural form of "feliz" (happy) and follows the rule of replacing "z" with "-ces".

43. La casa es bastante larga // My house is quiet large

✗ My house is quiet large = Mi casa es bastante <u>larga</u>.

✓ My house is quiet large = Mi casa es bastante <u>grande</u>.

The word "large" in English means, when describing an object, of considerable great size. Something large is something big.

On the other hand, "largo" in Spanish means long, meaning that it measures a great distance from one end to the other.

Therefore, "una casa larga" would be a very long house whereas a "large house" would be translated as "una casa grande".

44. En domingo normalmente juego al fútbol // On Sundays I normally play football

✗   On Sunday I normally play football = **En** domingo normalmente juego al fútbol.

✓   On Sunday I normally play football = **El** domingo normalmente juego al fútbol.

Sometimes, certain English words or expressions cannot be directly translated into Spanish because the two languages use different words or structures to convey a specific meaning. One clear example we have discussed before is when talking about age. In English, we say "I am 11 years old," but in Spanish, we would never say "Soy 11 años de viejo". Instead, we say "Tengo 11 años", which literally translates to "I have 11 years".

Another example is when ordering something. In English, we might say, "Can I have / Can I get x, please?" However, this cannot be translated directly into Spanish because we would never say "¿Puedo tener x, por favor?". In Spanish, we would say "Ponme un x, por favor," which translates literally to "Pour/Give me x, please".

This phenomenon is known as *collocation*, which refers to certain words that frequently occur together more often than would be expected by chance. Prepositions such as "on," "in," "at," "off," etc., are affected by collocation rules.

For example, "on" would be normally translated to "en". So, when we say "<u>on</u> the beach" , in Spanish, we would say "<u>en</u> la playa". However, "on" has various other translations as well. For instance, when we say "It's a book <u>on</u> orchids," it would be translated to "Es un libro <u>sobre</u> orquídeas" in Spanish.

Having this in mind, when we use the structure "on + days", in Spanish, we use "the + days". Something I advise my students to avoid mistakes when learning Spanish is to adjust their English to match Spanish structures. If you say "On Mondays I cook," you need to first adjust your English to match the Spanish structure and then translate. By doing it this way, you will never forget or be wrong!

For example, "On Mondays I cook" would be first rearranged in your head as "The Mondays I cook" and now we can translate literally into Spanish and it would be "Los lunes cocino".

<u>On</u> Mondays I cook - > **The** Mondays I cook -> **Los** lunes cocino.

45. ¿Puedo tener un café, por favor? // Can I have a coffee, please?

✗ Can I have a coffee, please? = ¿**Puedo tener** un café, por favor?

✓ Can I have a coffee, please? = ¿**Me pones** un café, por favor?

As outlined before, different languages have set phrases and sentences for certain situations. Did you know that in India people don't normally say "thank you"? It's more common that they express their gratitude through actions or gestures and saying thank you in some familiar contexts can be seen as overly formal. Ordering something is one of those situations where the language repertoire is quite narrow. When ordering a coffee or any beverage we would say in Spanish, literally, "Do you pour me a coffee/beer, please"?

Equally, when ordering, we use the *Imperative tense* in Spanish, but we show politeness by adding things like "por favor". So we would say "Ponme un café con leche, por favor (or simply: un café con leche, por favor)".

46. Me encanta mucho // I love it very much

✗   I love it very much = Me encanta **mucho**.

✓   I love it very much = Me encanta.

As outlined in mistake 44, this is a matter of *collocation*. When we say "me gusta", we can emphasise it by adding "mucho" or "un montón". However, when using "me encanta" which already means that you love something, we can't add "mucho" because it is already the highest degree of liking, so to speak. To express a higher degree, we would need to venture into the realm of poetry! *Oh la la*!

47. ¿Qué es tu número de teléfono? // What is your phone number?

✗   What is your phone number? = **¿Qué** es tu número de teléfono?

✓   What is your phone number? = **¿Cuál** es tu número de teléfono?

This is also another common *collocation* mistake (see mistake 44). There are several common questions where we use "what" in English but must change it to "which" in Spanish. Examples are:

- <u>What</u> is your name? = ¿~~Qué~~ <u>Cuál</u> es tu nombre?

- <u>What</u> is your address? = ¿~~Qué~~ <u>Cuál</u> es tu dirección?

- <u>What</u> is your favourite colour? = ¿~~Qué~~ <u>Cuál</u> es tu color favorito?

- <u>What</u> is your plan for today? = ¿~~Qué~~ <u>Cuál</u> es tu plan para hoy?

- <u>What</u> is your date of birth? ¿~~Qué~~ <u>Cuál</u> es tu fecha de nacimiento?

- <u>What</u> is your phone number? ¿~~Qué~~ <u>Cuál</u> es tu número de teléfono?

In general, we use "qué" when asking for general or broader definitions, descriptions or information. We use "cuál" when asking for specific information where the options are limited and the question is not open. If you think about it, all the questions I have used as examples are asking for something very specific. Examples of open questions:

What is love = ¿Qué es el amor?
What do you think? = ¿Qué piensas?
What do you feel? = ¿Qué sientes?

48. Tuve que preguntar por direcciones // I had to ask for directions

✗   I had to ask for directions = Tuve que **preguntar** por direcciones.

✓   I had to ask for directions = Tuve que **pedir** direcciones.

The verb "to ask" in Spanish is "preguntar". In English, "to ask <u>for</u>" something has a different meaning than just "to ask" something. Think of "to ask a person" or "to ask <u>for</u> a person".

To "ask for" is translated into Spanish as "pedir". Therefore, if we wanted to say, "Ask for help if you need it", we would say "Pide ayuda si la necesitas". Asking for directions would be "pedir direcciones".

49. Mi padre tiene no bigote // My dad has no moustache

✗ My dad has no moustache = Mi padre tiene **no** bigote.

✓ My dad has no moustache = Mi padre **no** tiene bigote.

In Spanish, negative particles like "not, no, isn't, ain't" always go <u>before the verb</u>. In this sentence the verb is "tiene", therefore we must place the "no" before the verb.

There are plenty of other examples where in English the negative particle goes after the verb. This is a very common mistake. Examples:

"Juan is **not** tall" would be translated into "Juan **no** <u>es</u> alto". ("Juan <u>es</u> **no** alto" would be wrong).

"José was **not** there" would be translated as "José **no** <u>estaba</u> allí". ("José <u>estaba</u> **no** allí" would be wrong).

50. Me gustaría casarse con un chico guapo // I would like to marry a handsome boy

✗ I would like to marry a handsome boy = Me gustaría **casarse** con un chico guapo.

✓ I would like to marry a handsome boy = Me gustaría **casarme** con un chico guapo.

"Casarse" (to marry, or to get married) is a reflexive verb. When we use the infinitive of a reflexive verb after another verb in the first person, we need to change the "-se" ending of the infinitive for "-me". For instance, if we wanted to say in Spanish "I don't want to get married", we would say "No quiero casar<u>me</u>". When using a different person of the verb, it follows the same pattern:

You don't want to get married: No quieres casar<u>te</u>.

However, if we are talking about the action itself without putting ourselves in the formula we would use the "-se" ending. For example, if we wanted to say "I think that getting married is expensive", we would say "Pienso que casarse es caro", because we are talking about the general action of getting married, without getting married ourselves.

With this in mind, let's see different sentences with different meanings:

Pienso que casar<u>se</u> es importante = I think that getting married is important.

Pienso que casar<u>te</u> es importante = I think that getting married (yourself) is important (or "I think that marrying you is important" as if I'm officiating the ceremony myself).

Piensas que casar<u>te</u> es importante = You think that getting married (yourself) is important.

Pienso que casar<u>me</u> es importante = I think that getting married (myself) is important.

If we wanted to say "I like to wake up early" we would say "Me gusta levantar<u>me</u> temprano" because you like to wake up early yourself. We are not talking about the general action of waking up early. If we wanted to say "I like the idea of waking up early" we would say "Me gusta la idea de levantar<u>se</u> temprano" as this doesn't imply you're doing it yourself necessarily.

51. Me llevo bien con mis abuelos porque es comprensivo // I get along with my grandparents because they are understanding

✗ I get along with my grandparents because they are understanding = Me llevo bien con mis abuelos porque **es** comprensivo.

✓ I get along with my grandparents because they are understanding = Me llevo bien con mis abuelos porque **son** comprensivos.

Oddly enough, I frequently come across this error where "es" and "son" are confused. We tend to forget that the subject in the sentece (abuelos) is plural and wrongly use "es" instead of "son".

Also, as a side note, "comprensivo" means understanding", not "comprehensive" as in wide scope. "Comprensivo" is related to comprehension, understanding.

52. Ayer usé mi móvil ver vídeos // Yesterday I used my phone to watch videos

✗ Yesterday I used my phone to watch videos = Ayer usé mi móvil ver vídeos.

✓ Yesterday I used my phone to watch videos = Ayer usé mi móvil **para** ver vídeos.

When translating from English to Spanish, you might know that "to watch" translates to "ver". However, you might wonder why we sometimes need to add "para" in Spanish. In Spanish grammar, there's a rule to remember: If you can add "in order to" before an infinitive in English and it still sounds correct, then you generally need to include "para" in the Spanish translation. This "para" serves the purpose of "in order to" or "for". Let's consider some examples:

"I study <u>to pass</u>". Can I add in order to before the <u>infinitive</u>?

I study (in order to) pass. Yes, I can! Then, I must add "para" when translating.

Estudio <u>para</u> aprobar.
I bought a new TV to watch the World Cup.
I bought a new TV (in order to) watch the World Cup.
Compré una tele nueva <u>para</u> ver el mundial.

If it doesn't sound right in English, then we don't need "para".

I don't want to smoke.
I don't want ~~(in order to)~~ smoke. (It doesn't sound right!)
No quiero fumar. (I don' need para).

53. He escribido una carta a la Reina // I have written a letter to the Queen

✗   I have written a letter to the Queen = He **escribido** una carta a la Reina.

✓   I have written a letter to the Queen = He **escrito** una carta a la Reina.

This is the sort of mistake that native Spanish-speaking children would make. Once your brain knows the pattern of the present perfect tense, where the past participle always ends in "-ido" or "-ado" we automatically think viv<u>ir</u> -> vivido, escribir -> escrib<u>ido</u>. However, escribir is irregular, like others, and its past participle would be *escrito*.

This is a list of other irregular ones:

Tener (to have) - Tenido (had)
Decir (to say) - Dicho (said)
Hacer (to do/make) - Hecho (done/made)

Ver (to see) - Visto (seen)

Abrir (to open) - Abierto (opened)

Romper (to break) - Roto (broken)

Poner (to put) - Puesto (put)

Morir (to die) - Muerto (died)

Resolver (to solve) - Resuelto (solved)

54. Estoy mirando por mis llaves // I am looking for my keys

✗ I am looking for my keys = Estoy **mirando** por mis llaves.

✓ I am looking for my keys = Estoy **buscando** mis llaves.

As outlined in mistake 45, in English, it is common to find that a little word acting as a preposition changes the meaning of a verb completely. Think of "to give" and "to give up". That little "up" totally changes the meaning of the verb. These are called *phrasal verbs* in English.

In Spanish, however, this rarely happens. Adding a preposition to a verb doesn't change the meaning. When we add a preposition to a verb in English and the meaning changes, we will have a completely different word in Spanish.

Examples:

To look = Mirar.

To look <u>for</u> = Buscar.

To give = Dar.

To give <u>up</u> = Abandonar.

To run = Correr.

To run <u>out</u> = Acabarse.

55. La gente son muy amables // People are very kind.

✘   People are very kind = La gente <u>son</u> muy amables.

✓   People are very kind = La gente <u>es</u> muy amable.

In Spanish, the word "gente" (which translates to "people") is treated as a singular entity, much like the English word "everybody". Consequently, when using "gente," you should use the third-person singular form of the verb. For example, "La gente es simpática," which translates to "People are nice," uses "es" (is) rather than a plural verb form.

In contrast, English treats "people" as a plural entity, so we say "People <u>are</u> nice" instead of "People <u>is</u> nice". In addition, English treats "everybody" as a singular entity, akin to how Spanish treats "gente". That's why in English, we say, "Everybody need_s_ love" or "Everybody _is_ here," using the singular form of the verb. It's worth noting that Spanish has another term for "people": "personas" which is treated as a plural entity, much like "people" in English. For instance:

"La <u>gente</u> <u>es</u> intrínsecamente egoísta" translates to "People are inherently selfish".

"Las <u>personas</u> <u>son</u> intrínsecamente egoístas" translates to "People are inherently selfish".

56. Este libro es mucho interesante // This book is very interesting

✗   This book is very interesting = Este libro es **mucho** interesante.

✓   This book is very interesting = Este libro es **muy** interesante.

We tend to mistake "mucho" for "muy" and vice versa. Is it maybe because they both start with an m? Remember,

muy = very.
mucho = much or a lot.

57. No problema // No problem

✗   No problem = No problema.

✓   No problem = No **hay** problema.

In Spanish, we say something similar to "no problem" , "There is no problem = No hay problema".

58. Tomé a mi hermana al aeropuerto // I took my sister to the airport.

✗   I took my sister to the airport = **Tomé** a mi hermana al aeropuerto.

✓   I took my sister to the airport = **Llevé** a mi hermana al aeropuerto.

Sometimes, when we use a verb in English in a given situation, in Spanish we use a different one and vice-versa. This is one of those cases. When talking about transport and giving someone a lift we use the verb "llevar" in Spanish (to take, to carry, to wear). We would not use the verb "tomar" which can also mean "to take", "to have", etc.

Examples:

The taxi <u>took</u> my aunt home = El taxi <u>llevó</u> a mi tia a casa.
I <u>took</u> my dog to the vet = <u>Llevé</u> a mi perro al veterinario.

These are some examples with the verb "tomar" in Spanish:

Me gustaría tomar café =I would like to have coffee.
No me gusta tomar decisiones = I don't like to make/ take decisions.
Tomo el sol = I sunbathe (literally "I take the sun").
Voy a tomar el autobús = I am going to take the bus.
Tomó medidas para proteger el pueblo = He took measures to protect the town.

Note that when we say in English "I had breakfast" we say in Spanish "Tomé el desayuno" (literally I took breakfast), instead of "Tuve (I had) breakfast". In Spanish we use the verb "tomar" (to take) with food whereas in English we use "tener" (to have).

I have chicken for lunch = Tomo pollo para la comida.
For dinner, I had fish = Para la cena tomé pollo.

Finally, when speaking someone could say something in Spanish like:

"¿Qué tienes hoy para cenar? Tengo pollo hoy, ¿y tú?
= What do you have today for dinner? I have chicken today, and you?"

To avoid any confusion, you can always use the verb "comer" (Ayer comí pescado en el desayuno = Yesterday I had fish for breakfast).

59. Me gustan acción películas // I like action films.

✗ I like action films = Me gustan **acción películas**.

✓ I like action films = Me gustan **las películas de acción**.

Amigo! remember that adjectives go after nouns in Spanish. The word action describes the kind of film, so "acción" needs to go after the noun.

On top of that, with "horror films" we would say "películas <u>de</u> terror", not "terror películas". There are plenty of situations where we find the structure "noun + de + adjective" when in English we have "adjective + noun".

These are the most common ones:

Possession. When we have "'s" in English.

My brother's bedroom = La habitación de mi hermano. My mum's car = El coche de mi madre.

Characteristic of an object/thing. To indicate what something is made of.

A silver ring = Un anillo de plata.

An apple juice = Un zumo de manzana.

A 12-years-old boy = Un niño de 12 años.

This striped shirt = Esta camiseta de rayas.

A strawberry ice cream = Un helado de fresa.

A Christmas meal = Una comida de Navidad.

A Spanish lesson = Una clase de español.

A German teacher = Un profesor de alemán.

A plastic cup = Un vaso de plástico.

60. Mi madre siempre me soporta en mis decisiones // My mother always supports me in my decisions.

✗ My mother always supports me in my decisions.
Mi madre siempre me **soporta** en mis decisiones.

✓ My mother always supports me in my decisions.
Mi madre siempre me **apoya** en mis decisiones.

"Soportar" in Spanish means "to hold", "to carry" or "to bear". It also means to stand something/someone.

Examples:

No soporto las colas = I can't stand queues.
Las columnas soportan el tejado = The columns support the roof.

"Soportar" does not have the meaning of helping or backing someone or something up. Instead, we use "apoyar". Interestingly, "apoyarse en" is used when talking about relying on something/someone.

<u>Apoyo</u> la decision = I <u>support</u> the decision.
<u>Me apoyo</u> en mi madre = <u>I rely</u> on my mum.

Finally, "apoyarse en" also means "to rest" or "lean on" something physically.

No te apoyes en la pared = Do not lean on the wall.
El techo se apoya en las columnas = The roof rests on the columns.

Finally, we could also use "descansar" (to rest) in the same way and say "El techo descansa en las columnas", which conveys the message in a more poetic way.

61. El chico vivo con es muy sucio // The guy I live with is very dirty

✗ The guy I live with is very dirty = El chico **vivo con** es muy sucio.

✓ The guy I live with is very dirty = El chico **con quien** vivo es muy sucio.

Whenever we have a preposition <u>at the end of a sentence</u> like in "The guy I live <u>with</u>" or "Spain is the country she comes <u>from</u>" or "Money is the reason she is known <u>for</u>", we need to change the sentence as follows:

The guy I live <u>with</u> = The guy <u>with whom</u> I live.
Spain is the country she comes <u>from</u> = Spain is the country <u>from where</u> she comes.
Money is the reason she is known <u>for</u> = Money is the reason <u>for what</u> she is known.

Remember that, in English, ending a sentence with a preposition is sometimes frowned upon in a more formal context. In Spanish, we couldn't translate literally if a preposition is at the end of the sentence, but once the preposition is moved to agree with the so-attributed, Winston Churchill's observation, we could translate:

The guy <u>with whom</u> I live = El chico <u>con quién</u> vivo.

Spain is the country <u>from</u> <u>where</u> she comes = España es el país <u>de</u> <u>donde</u> viene.

Money is the reason <u>for</u> <u>which</u> she is known = El dinero es la razón <u>por</u> <u>la cual</u> es conocida.

62. Te veo en la mañana // See you in the morning

✘   See you in the morning = Te veo <u>**en**</u> la mañana.

✓   See you in the morning = Te veo <u>**por**</u> la mañana.

When referring to the different parts of the day we use certain prepositions . In English, we say "<u>**in**</u> the morning", "<u>**in**</u> the evening" but would normally say "<u>**at**</u> night", not "<u>**in**</u> the night" which sounds much more poetic and is very rarely used.

In the same way, we could say "<u>en</u> la mañana" and it sounds poetic, but the right way to say "in the morning" would be "<u>por</u> la mañana".

In the morning = Por la mañana.
At midday/at noon = Al mediodía.
In the afternoon/evening = Por la tarde.
At night = Por la noche.
At midnight = A medianoche.

63. Soy un cocinero // I am a chef

✖ I am a chef = Soy **un** cocinero

✓ I am a chef = Soy cocinero

This is an easy one. I remember when I learned it in English. In English we say "I am **a** chef" but in Spanish, we say "I am chef", without the "a". It always works like this with professions.

I am a doctor = Soy doctor.
I am a nurse = Soy enfermero.
I am a politician = Soy político.

64. Mi hermano está embarazado // My brother is embarrased

✖ My brother is embarrased = Mi hermano está **embarazado**.

✓ My brother is embarrased = Mi hermano está **avergonzado**.

"Embarazado" is a *false friend* for English speakers. It means "pregnant", and it always ends with an "a", "embarazad<u>a</u>". It looks like "embarrassed" but nothing could be further away from the correct meaning of the word!

65. Me duelen mis ojos // My eyes hurt

✘   My eyes hurt = Me duelen **mis** ojos.

✓   My eyes hurt = Me duelen <u>los</u> ojos.

Muy interesante this one! We always refer to our body in English with "my": <u>my</u> head, <u>my</u> fingers, <u>my</u> belly. In Spanish whenever we talk about the human body, even if it's to describe pain or any other sensations, we use "the":

Me duele <u>la</u> barriga = <u>My</u> belly hurts.
Tengo <u>las</u> piernas cansadas: <u>My</u> legs are tired.
<u>My</u> molars are numb = Tengo <u>las</u> muelas dormidas.
I have a wound on <u>my</u> arm = Tengo una herida en <u>el</u> brazo.

66. Hago muchos errores cuando hablo español // I make many mistakes when I speak Spanish

✗ I make many mistakes when I speak Spanish
   <u>Hago</u> muchos errores cuando hablo español.

✓ I make many mistakes when I speak Spanish
   <u>Tengo</u> muchos errores cuando hablo español.

Again, this mistake occurs when translating literally. In Spanish we don't "make mistakes", we "have" them.

It is interesting that literal translations contribute to the evolution of languages, especially now that we use the internet and are bombarded with viral memes. Sometimes, when I listen to or read American English, I see loanwords or expressions that have been literally taken from Spanish. For instance, things like "hasta la vista". Recently I have been playing Pokemon Violet, with the language set in American English, and I was really surprised to see tons of Spanish expressions in the dialogues like "perfecto, hasta la visa, vamos, hola, amigo, tarde, etc".

Think of the amount of people who speak Spanish in the USA (around 41 million). Some states in the US have more Spanish speakers than English speakers! For those people, Spanish is their mother tongue and English their second language.

The way I see it is that sometimes they can translate something literally which, by chance, English native speakers find funny, exotic or whatever and they repeat it. This becomes viral, people start using it and it is incorporated into English from Spanish.

67. Voy a tomar un otro bocadillo // I'm gonna have another roll/sandwich

✗ I'm gonna have another roll = Voy a tomar **un** otro bocadillo.

✓ I'm gonna have another roll = Voy a tomar otro bocadillo .

If you wish to order the same delicious sandwich again, you should use "otro", not "un otro". This mistake likely occurs because people break down the word "another" into its constituent parts: "an" (which translates to "un/una") and "other" (which translates to "otro"). As a result, they end up translating "another" as "un otro".

In addition, the use of "other" and "another" can be confusing when translating from Spanish into English. To help clarify, let's see some examples:

Este es el otro coche = This is the other car.

Necesito otro coche = I need another car.

La otra asignatura = The other subject.

Otra asignatura me mataría = Another subject would kill me.

As you can see, normally we use "otro" (otra/otros/otras) when we have "the" in English. We would never say "un otro".

68. Esto no hace sentido // This doesn't make sense

✘   This doesn't make sense = Esto no **hace** sentido.

✓   This doesn't make sense = Esto no **tiene** sentido.

I remember my first week in England, back in my 20s. I told a flatmate*: "This doesn't have sense". He looked at me and replied, "You mean it doesn't make sense, right?".

Sometimes, English offers some flexibility in translation. For example, in Spanish, we say "tomar una decisión", and in English, you can say either "to take a decision" or "to make a decision". However, in the case of making sense, we can only translate it as "tiene sentido" in Spanish, which literally means "have sense".

Lo que dices no <u>tiene</u> ningún sentido = What you say doesn't <u>make</u> any sense.

Thank you for your valuable lessons, dear flatmate!

69. Estamos esperando por el autobús // We're waiting for the bus

✗ We're waiting for the bus = Estamos esperando **por** el autobús.

✓ We're waiting for the bus = Estamos esperando el autobús.

The verb "esperar" doesn't need a preposition with it. When we want to specify what we are waiting for, we would just use "esperar + object". However, there is an exception. When we wait for <u>someone</u>, then we use "esperar + <u>a</u>". We also use it when there is a second verb.

I'm waiting for my food = Estoy esperando mi comida.
I'm waiting for my <u>mum</u> = Estoy esperando <u>a</u> mi <u>madre</u>.
She's waiting for her <u>dog</u> = Está esperando <u>a</u> su perro.
I'm waiting for my food <u>to come</u> = Estoy esperando <u>a</u> que mi comida <u>venga</u>.
You're waiting for the temperature <u>to go down</u> = Estás esperando <u>a</u> que las temperaturas <u>bajen</u>.

70. Mi móvil no trabaja // My phone doesn't work

✖   My phone doesn't work = Mi móvil no **trabaja**.

✓   My phone doesn't work = Mi móvil no **funciona**.

In English, we have something similar to "funcionar": to function. We could say that my phone doesn't function but would usually say that it doesn't work. This mistake is easy to avoid if we remember this. We would never use the verb "trabajar" when referring to something not working, but always the verb "funcionar".

My car doesn't <u>work</u> = Mi coche no <u>funciona</u>.

This strategy doesn't <u>work</u> = Esta estrategia no <u>funciona</u>.

71. Ayer tuve un montón de divertido en la fiesta // Yesterday I had a lot of fun at the party.

✗ Yesterday I had a lot of fun at the party = Ayer tuve un montón de **divertido** en la fiesta.

✓ Yesterday I had a lot of fun at the party = Ayer tuve un montón de **diversión** en la fiesta.

"Divertido" is one of the first words people learn in Spanish. "Divertido" is an adjective and it means both "fun" and "funny" when describing someone or something. However, when we use "fun" as a noun, like in "I do it for fun" (note that fun is not describing any nouns here), the translation in Spanish is "diversión".

In this case, when we say "I had a lot of fun", we are using "fun" as a noun, therefore we would need to use "diversión".

Maybe you have seen a Spaniard taking a picture of one of those road signs that have the word "diversion" with an arrow on them. When I used to see them when I first came to England I thought "oh, this is where the fun is!". *Follow the arrow!*

By the way, "diversion" in English is translated in Spanish as "desvío".

En la calle hay un desvío = There is a diversion on the street.

72. Fui a Francia tres tiempos el año pasado // I went to France three times last year

✗ I went to France three times last year = Fui a Francia tres **tiempos** el año pasado.

✓ I went to France three times last year = Fui a Francia tres **veces** el año pasado.

I see my pupils struggle with this one. The word "vez" in Spanish means "time", but not as in "tiempo". It means "time" as in one time, two times, three times.

Example:

Tomar la pastilla una vez al día = Take the tablet once a day.

Then the plural of "vez" is "veces" because when we want to make a "–z" ending word plural, we swap that "-z" for "-ces" (feliz -> felices, pez-> peces).

This way we have the very common expression "a veces" (sometimes). Unfortunately, we don't have the words "once" or "twice" in Spanish, so we would always need to translate them into one time (una vez), two times (dos veces), etc.

Me ducho dos veces al día = I shower twice (two times) a day.

73. El más aprendo el más me gusta // The more I learn the more I like it

✗ The more I learn the more I like it = <u>El</u> más aprendo <u>el</u> más me gusta.

✓ The more I learn the more I like it = **Cuanto** más aprendo más me gusta.

This is a structure, again, that works differently in both languages. Luckily ,the structure in English "The more/less A, the more/less B" can be replicated in Spanish with a couple of tweaks: "Cuanto más/menos A, más/menos B".

Let's see a couple of examples:

The more	I know you	the more	I like you
Cuanto más	te conozco	más	me gustas

The less	I know	the happier	I am
Cuanto menos	sé	más feliz	soy

74. Mi madre quiere yo estudio 3 horas al día // My mum wants me to study 3 hours a day!

✗ My mum wants me to study 3 hours a day! = Mi madre quiere <u>yo estudio</u> 3 horas al día.

✓ My mum wants me to study 3 hours a day! = Mi madre quiere <u>que estudie</u> 3 horas al día.

Whenever we encounter a sentence structure where someone wants someone else to do something, or wants a particular event to happen, we need to use the subjunctive mood. This is because the subjunctive is used to express hypothetical situations, desires, or things that have not yet occurred.

My aunt doesn't want it to happen = Mi tía no quiere que pase.

My dad would like me to wash the car = A mi padre le gustaría que lave el coche.

This is one of those cases where we use the subjunctive after "que".

75. Mi hermano llamó mi madre una idiota // My brother called my mum an idiot

✗ My brother called my mum an idiot = Mi hermano llamó a mi madre <u>una</u> idiota.

✓ My brother called my mum an idiot = Mi hermano llamó a mi madre idiota.

We use in Spanish the same kind of sentence, but Spanish admits another word order. In this way, we could say "Mi hermano llamó idiota a mi madre. What is different is that in Spanish we omit the article "a". Therefore, we would not say "una idiota", bust just "idiota". Let's see other examples:

My sister called me stupid = Mi hermana me llamó estúpido.

My classmate called him fat = Mi compañero le llamó gordo.

My brother called me a monster = Mi hermano me llamó monstruo.

My brother called my friend silly = Mi hermano llamó tonta a mi amiga or Mi hermano llamó a mi amiga tonta.

76. Ten cuidado cuando viajando con lluvia fuerte // Take care when travelling in heavy rain.

✗ Take care when travelling in heavy rain = Ten cuidado cuando **viajando** con lluvia fuerte.

✓ Take care when travelling in heavy rain = Ten cuidado cuando **viajes** con lluvia fuerte.

In English, there's a structure that uses "when" followed by a verb ending in "-ing' (e.g., when singing, when talking, when entering). This specific structure doesn't have a direct equivalent in Spanish. When translating such sentences into Spanish, we generally use the present tense. For example:

When speaking a foreign language what matters is communication = Cuando hablas un idioma extranjero lo que importa es la comunicación.

77. Puedo hablar con mis amigos quien viven muy lejos // I can talk to my friends who live far away.

✗ I can talk to my friends who live far away = Puedo hablar con mis amigos **quien** viven muy lejos.

✓ I can talk to my friends who live far away = Puedo hablar con mis amigos **que** viven muy lejos.

We tend to mix up "quien" and "que" as they are used in slightly different ways in Spanish and English. When we have "who" in English in a sentence <u>without prepositions</u>, we will always translate it for "que". If we have a preposition like "with" (con) in the sentence we translate it for "quién".

<u>Que- When we have no prepositions:</u>

My mum, <u>who</u> is a lawyer, earns a lot = Mi madre, <u>que</u> es abogada, gana un montón.

He is the person <u>who</u> owns the land = El es la persona <u>que</u> posee la tierra.

<u>Quien- When we have a preposition:</u>

She is the lady I work <u>with</u> = Ella es la persona <u>con</u> <u>quién</u> trabajo.

Who are you going <u>with</u>? = ¿<u>Con</u> <u>quién</u> vas?

She is the person <u>with</u> <u>whom</u> I live = Ella es la persona <u>con</u> <u>quién</u> vivo.

78. Pareces guapa // You look beautiful

✘   You look beautiful = **<u>Pareces</u>** guapa.

✓   You look beautiful = **<u>Estás</u>** guapa.

This is an interesting example and it links again with "ser" and "estar". "Parecer" means "to look like" but its meaning has a subtle difference in Spanish. If we said "pareces guapa" that would mean that we are not sure. It *seems* to be the case that you look beautiful, but we are not totally sure. It only *seems* so. On the other hand, "estás guapa" means that you look beautiful, then and there. Maybe you see your sister in a new beautiful dress and you say "¡Qué guapa estás!".

On the other hand, "Eres guapa" means that you are beautiful. You've been gifted with beauty by the Gods!

I have a funny anecdote about this one. One day my friend Emma from Sheffield came to visit me in Murcia (Spain). My mum at the time was learning English. Emma took like 2 hours in the bathroom to get ready, putting her make-up on, dressing, etc. When she came out my mum said "Oh, you are beautiful". Emma smiled and said "thank you, you too".

What mum said was incorrect, as she thought in her head "qué guapa <u>estás</u>", but she translated literally and forgot that "estar" is temporary, and therefore she should have said "Oh, you look beautiful".*

Note for Emma: Emma eres muy guapa, pero cuando haces tu ritual de belleza ¡estás aún más guapa! x (Emma says that her ritual took only 1.5h, not 2!).

79. Viví aquí para dos años // I lived here for two years

✗ I lived here for two years = Viví aquí **para** dos años.

✓ I lived here for two years = Viví aquí **durante** dos años.

The mistake here is related to the preposition used to express a period of time. In English, we use "for" to express a duration, such as "for two years" or "for a week". In Spanish, the appropriate preposition is "durante". We could also say "viví aquí <u>por</u> dos años".

Never use "para" (which is another translation of the word "for") in this context as it implies purpose or an intended recipient, not duration.

80. Si habría estudiado más, habría aprobado el examen // If I had studied more, I would have passed the exam.

✗ If I had studied more, I would have passed the exam = Si **habría** estudiado más, habría aprobado el examen.

✓ If I had studied more, I would have passed the exam = Si **hubiera** estudiado más, habría aprobado el examen.

In Spanish, "hubiera" and "habría" are both forms of the conditional perfect tense, which is used to express actions that would have taken place under certain conditions in the past. However, they are used in slightly different contexts:

"Hubiera" (or "hubiese") is the past subjunctive form of the verb "haber" combined with the past participle of another verb. It's used to express a hypothetical or unrealised action that would have occurred in the past. It's often used after "si" (if).

"Habría" is the conditional form of the verb "haber" combined with the past participle of another verb. It's used to express a hypothetical or future action that would happen under a certain condition. It's often used to express possibilities, predictions, or potential outcomes.

Example:

Si estudias más, habría mejores resultados = If you study more, there would be better results.

In summary, "hubiera" (or "hubiese") is used for counterfactual or unrealized past conditions, while "habría" is used for hypothetical or potential future conditions. The choice between the two depends on whether you're discussing a past situation that didn't happen or a future situation that might happen.

If I had bought a lottery ticket, I would have won the lottery = Si hubiera comprado un billete de lotería habría ganado la lotería.

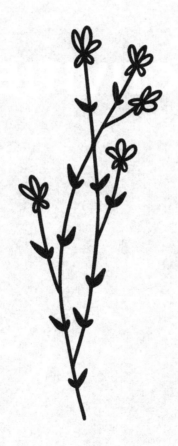

ACTIVITIES

Activity 1

Fill in the Gaps. Fill in the blanks with the correct word or phrase:

1. Soy _____ (good) en matemáticas.
2. Tengo _____ (the) ojos azules.
3. Es un hombre _____ (unfortunate/pitiable).
4. Juegas al fútbol muy _____ (well).
5. Me gusta porque _____ (it is) interesante.

Activity 2

Correct the Mistake. Read the sentences and correct the mistake in each sentence:

1. Soy bien al baloncesto.
2. Tengo azules pelo.
3. Tengo un grande coche.
4. Inglaterra es cerca de España.
5. Tú escribes la carta muy bien.
6. Me gusta porque es no aburrido.
7. Actualmente, no tengo idea.
8. Es el más emocionante película que he visto.

Activity 3

Translate. Translate the following English sentences into Spanish:

1. I am good at tennis.
2. I have green eyes.
3. I have black hair.
4. I have a big family.
5. France is close to Germany.
6. She sings the song very well.
7. I like it because it is funny.
8. Actually, I'm not sure.
9. It's the most beautiful city I've visited.

Activity 4

Choose the Correct Option. Choose the right translation for each sentence:

1. I am good at dancing.

    a.) Soy bien en baile.

    b.) Soy bueno en baile.

2. She has brown eyes.

    a.) Ella tiene los ojos marrones.

    b.) Ella tiene marrones ojos.

3. He is a kind man.

    a.) Es un amable hombre.

    b.) Es un hombre amable.

4. You write letters very well.

    a.) Tú escribes cartas muy bien.

    b.) Escribes cartas muy bien.

5. It's the least interesting book.

    a.) Es el libro menos interesante.

    b.) Es el menos interesante libro.

Activity 5

True or False. Determine whether the statement is true or false based on the lessons from the book:

- In Spanish, the adjective usually goes before the noun. (T/F)

- "Actualmente" means "currently" in Spanish. (T/F)

- "Soy bueno al fútbol" is the correct way to say "I am good at football" in Spanish. (T/F)

- The verb "estar" is used when talking about location. (T/F)

- The *zero copula* is frequently used in Spanish. (T/F)

Activity 6

Word Bank: Using the word bank, complete the sentences with the most appropriate term.

Word Bank: [mayor, antiguo, hay, hace, viejo, lloviendo, nieva]

1. En mi familia, mi primo Carlos es el _____.

2. Mi reloj es muy _____; era de mi abuelo.

3. No puedes salir sin paraguas porque está _____.

4. _____ tres lápices en mi bolsa.

5. El edificio _____ es un museo ahora.

6. En invierno, en las montañas, a menudo _____.

Activity 7

Underline the Mistake. Underline the
mistake in each sentence and correct it.

1. Hay es 4 manzanas en la mesa.
2. Mi hermana más joven es muy inteligente.
3. La casa es muy anciana y necesita reparaciones.
4. Es mucho frío por la noche.

Activity 8

Multiple Choice. Circle the correct translation.

1. It's very hot.

    a) Es mucho calor.

    b) Hace mucho calor.

    c) Es mucho caliente.

2. The former director is here.

    a) El antiguo director está aquí.

    b) El director viejo está aquí.

    c) El director anterior está aquí.

Activity 9

**Sentence Creation. Use the given words to
create a meaningful sentence.**

1. (libro / antiguo / muy / es / el)
2. (Juan / mayor / es/ hermano / mi)
3. (Hace / viento / hoy / mucho)
4. (es / Pedro / antiguo / muy)

Activity 10

Story Error Identification. Read the short story and underline any mistakes related to the language structures discussed. Then, correct them.

"Es un día soleado. Hace es calor. Mariana y su hermano más viejo, Carlos, deciden visitar un museo. El museo es muy anciano y tiene muchos artefactos antiguos".

Activity 11

Mistake Correction. Circle the mistake in each sentence and write the correct form on the line.

1. Me jugar fútbol. _____

2. Me comer pollo. _____

3. Me prefiero comer la pizza. _____

4. Me gusta café porque es sano. _____

5. Estoy en amor con mi novio. _____

Activity 12

**Fill in the Blanks with Reflexive Pronouns.
Fill in each blank with the appropriate
reflexive pronoun (me, te, se, nos, os, se).**

1. _____ llamo Juan.
2. Ellos _____ visten rápidamente.
3. Tú _____ bañas cada noche.
4. Nosotros _____ peinamos en el baño.

Activity 13

Translate the Sentences. Translate the
following English sentences to Spanish,
considering the mistakes discussed.

1. I like dogs.
2. I prefer to drink tea.
3. He talks to himself.
4. You like to dance.
5. We are in love with the city.

1. _____

_____

2. _____

_____

3. _____

_____

4. _____

_____

Activity 14

Matching Activity. Match the sentence on the left with its correct translation on the right.

Me gusta el té	I prefer
Te hablo	Te duchas
Prefiero	I talk to you
Me encanta la música	Music fascinates me
You shower	I like tea

Activity 15

Gustar Sentences. Using the verb "gustar,"
write five sentences about things or
activities you like or dislike. Remember to
use "the".

1. _____
   _____
   _____

2. _____
   _____
   _____

3. _____
   _____
   _____

4. _____
   _____
   _____

5. _____
   _____
   _____

Activity 16

True or False. State if the translation is correct (True) or incorrect (False):

1. He was in the cinema = Estuvo en el cine.
2. What is your name? = ¿Qué es tu nombre?
3. I had to ask for directions = Tuve que preguntar por direcciones.
4. My dad has no beard = Mi padre tiene no barba.
5. She feels like eating = Siente como comer.

The 80 Most Common Mistakes in Spanish

Activity 17

Fill in the Blanks with the Correct Verb Form. Choose the right verb form to complete the sentences:

1. Ayer usé mi móvil para _____ (ver) vídeos.

2. Me gustaría _____ (casarse) con alguien especial.

3. Tengo ganas de _____ (ir) al parque.

4. No sé qué _____ (hacer) mañana.

5. ¿____ (estar) listo para la reunión?

Activity 18

Translate from English to Spanish.
Translate the following sentences:

1. How are you feeling today?
2. I don't know what to say.
3. What is your address?
4. I have to buy a new dress.
5. She was at the beach last weekend.

Activity 19

Fill in the Blanks with "Qué" or "Cuál".

1. _____ es tu plan para el fin de semana?

2. _____ es tu dirección?

3. _____ piensas de la película?

4. _____ es tu color favorito?

5. _____ es la razón de tu visita?

Activity 20

Match the English phrasal verb to its corresponding Spanish verb.

English	Spanish
a) To give up	1) Correr
b) To run	2) Abandonar
c) To look for	3) Mirar
d) To look	4) Acabarse
e) To run out	5) Buscar

The 80 Most Common Mistakes in Spanish

Activity 21

Decide which version of the sentence is correct.

1. Ellos son 16 años.
2. Ellos tienen 16 años.

1. Me gusta el vino blanco.
2. Me gusta vino blanco.

1. Mi hermano está embarazado.
2. Mi hermano está avergonzado.

1. Tengo frío en mis pies.
2. Tengo frío en los pies.

1. Hago pocos errores cuando hablo español.
2. Tengo pocos errores cuando hablo español.

Activity 22

Fill in the Blanks Directions: Fill in the blanks with the correct word from the given options.

1. Me duele ___ (mi/la) cabeza.

2. Mi móvil no _____(funciona/trabaja).

3. Tengo un montón de _____(divertido/ diversión).

4. Cuanto más _____(estudias, aprendes), más _____ (aprendo, estudias).

5. Ayer _____ (tuve/tenía) un montón de diversión en la fiesta.

Activity 23

Correct the Mistakes. Rewrite the following sentences correctly.

1. Estamos esperando por la comida.
2. Fui a Italia dos tiempos este verano.
3. Me duelen mis manos.
4. Ayer tuve un montón de divertido.

Activity 24

Translate into Spanish: Translate the following English sentences into Spanish.

1. My phone doesn't work.
2. The more I read, the more I understand.
3. My head hurts.
4. I'm waiting for my friend.
5. My feet are cold.

Activity 25

Fun with False Friends: Write down the English meanings of the following Spanish words that can be easily misinterpreted.

1. Embarazada: _____.

2. Diversión: _____.

3. Actualmente: _____.

4. Asistir: _____.

5. Sano: _____.

Activity 26

Choose the Correct Translation. Choose the best translation for the English sentences:

My teacher wants me to practise more.

    a) Mi profesor quiere yo practico más.
    b) Mi profesor quiere que practique más.

She called her brother lazy.

    a) Ella llamó perezoso a su hermano.
    b) Ella llamó un perezoso a su hermano.

Be careful when walking on the street.

    a) Ten cuidado cuando caminando en la calle.
    b) Ten cuidado cuando camines por la calle.

I know a man who can help you.

    a) Conozco a un hombre quien puede ayudarte.
    b) Conozco a un hombre que puede ayudarte.

You look tired.

    a) Pareces cansado.
    b) Estás cansado.

Activity 27

Underline the right answer from the options provided:

1. Mi prima quiere que yo (canta/cante) en la boda.

2. Mi amigo me llamó (tonto/un tonto).

3. Siempre sonríe cuando (trabajando/trabaja) con niños.

4. Ella es la chica con (quien/que) salí ayer.

5. Hoy (eres/estás) muy feliz.

Activity 28

True or False. Determine if the given translations are true (correct) or false (incorrect):

1. My friend wants me to come early. -> Mi amigo quiere que venga temprano. (True/False)

2. He called me a genius. -> Él me llamó un genio. (True/False)

3. Be careful when driving at night. -> Ten cuidado cuando conduciendo de noche. (True/False)

4. That's the guy who helped me. -> Ese es el chico quien me ayudó. (True/False)

5. You look upset. -> Pareces molesto. (True/False)

Activity 29

Matching. Match the English sentence to its correct Spanish counterpart:

My cousin would like me to visit her.	A mi prima le gustaría que la visite.
She called me intelligent.	Siempre estoy feliz cuando canto.
I'm always happy when singing.	Ella es la persona con quién hablé.
She is the person with whom I spoke.	Me llamó inteligente.
You look fantastic.	Estás fantástico.

Activity 30

Sentence Correction. Correct the mistakes in the following Spanish sentences:

1. Mi jefe quiere yo trabajar más tarde.

2. Mi hermana me llamó bonita a mí.

3. Cuida tus pasos cuando corriendo.

4. Él es el chico quien me vendió el coche.

5. Hoy eres muy animado.

ANSWERS

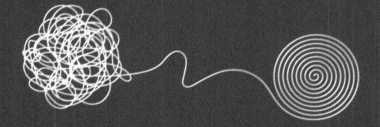

Activity 1

Fill in the Gaps.

1. Soy **bueno** en matemáticas.

   Explanation: When talking about being good at something, "bueno" is used.

2. Tengo **los** ojos azules.

   Explanation: We always put "los" before "ojos"in Spanish.

3. Es un hombre **pobre**.

   Explanation: "Pobre hombre" means pitiable or unfortunate man.

4. Juegas al fútbol muy **bien**.

   Explanation: We use "bien" to describe the verb (you play very **well**).

5. Me gusta porque **es** interesante.

   Explanation: The verb "**es**" is required here for the sentence to be grammatically correct.

Activity 2

Correct the Mistake.

1. Soy <u>bueno</u> en baloncesto. "Bueno" is used as "bien" means well and is an adverb.

2. Tengo <u>el</u> pelo azul. Remember: I have THE hair blue.

3. Tengo un coche <u>grande</u>. Adjectives go after nouns in Spanish.

4. Inglaterra <u>está</u> cerca de España. "Estar" is used for locations.

5. Escribes la carta muy bien. In Spanish we ommit pronouns.

6. Me gusta porque <u>no</u> es aburrido. "Not" always goes before the verb in Spanish.

7. <u>En realidad</u>, no tengo idea. "Actualmente" means "currently".

8. Es la película más emocionante que he visto. Consider word order and adjectival agreement.

Activity 3

Translate.

1. I am good at tennis = Soy bueno al tenis.
2. I have green eyes = Tengo los ojos verdes.
3. I have black hair = Tengo el pelo negro.
4. I have a big family = Tengo una familia grande.
5. France is close to Germany = Francia está cerca de Alemania.
6. She sings the son very well = Canta la canción muy bien.
7. I like it because it's funny = Me gusta porque es divertido.
8. Actually, I am not sure = En realidad, no estoy seguro.
9. It's the most beautiful city I've visited = Es la ciudad más bonita que he visitado.

Activity 4

Choose the Correct Option

I.   I am good at dancing.

    a.) Soy bien en baile.

    b.) <u>Soy bueno en baile.</u>

Explanation: "Bueno" means "good", "bien" means "well". We are "good" at something, not "well".

2.   She has brown eyes.

    a.) <u>Ella tiene los ojos marrones.</u>

    b.) Ella tiene marrones ojos.

Explanation: Remember the structure "She has THE eyes brown".

3.   He is a kind man.

    a.) Es un amable hombre.

    b.) <u>Es un hombre amable.</u>

Explanation: The adjective "amable" follows the noun "hombre" as adjectives go after nouns in Spanish.

4.   You write letters very well.

    a.) Tú escribes cartas muy bien.

b.) <u>Escribes cartas muy bien.</u>

Explanation: We omit pronouns in Spanish, so "tú" is not needed.

5. It's the least interesting book.

    a.) <u>Es el libro menos interesante.</u>
    b.) Es el menos interesante libro.

Explantion: This is the right structure for a comparison.

Activity 5

True or False Answers

1. In Spanish, the adjective usually goes before the noun. <u>False</u>.

   Explanation: In Spanish, the adjective usually goes after the noun.

2. "Actualmente" means "currently" in Spanish. <u>True</u>.

   Explanation: "Actualmente" translates to "currently".

3. "Soy bueno al fútbol" is the correct way to say "I am good at football" in Spanish. <u>True.</u>

   Explanation: "Soy bueno <u>en</u> futbol" is also correct.

4. The verb "estar" is used when talking about location. <u>True.</u>

   Explanation: "Estar" is used for locations and temporary states.

5. The zero copula is frequently used in Spanish. <u>False.</u>

   Explanation: The zero copula is not a frequent structure in Spanish.

Activity 6

Word Bank

1. En mi familia, mi primo Carlos es el <u>mayor</u>.

   Explanation: We use "mayor" to describe someone as older/oldest in the context of family relationships.

2. Mi reloj es muy <u>antiguo</u>; era de mi abuelo.

   Explanation: "Antiguo" is used to describe objects that are very old, like antiques. We could have used "viejo" as well.

3. No puedes salir sin paraguas porque está <u>lloviendo</u>.

   Explanation: The correct term for "it's raining" is "está lloviendo".

4. <u>Hay</u> tres lápices en mi bolsa.

   Explanation: The correct construction for "there are" in Spanish is "hay".

5. El edificio <u>viejo</u> es un museo ahora.

   Explanation: "Viejo" can be used to describe something as old, including buildings.

6. En invierno, en las montañas, a menudo <u>nieva</u>.

Explanation: The verb "nieva" translates to "it snows" in English.

Activity 7

Underline the Mistake

1. Hay <u>es</u> 4 manzanas en la mesa. → Hay 4 manzanas en la mesa.

   Explanation: The construction "hay es" is incorrect. The correct term is "hay".

2. Mi hermana <u>más joven</u> es muy inteligente. → Mi hermana <u>menor</u> es muy inteligente.

   Explanation: We use "menor" to refer to younger siblings in Spanish.

3. La casa es muy <u>anciana</u> y necesita reparaciones. → La casa es muy <u>vieja</u> y necesita reparaciones.

   Explanation: "Anciano/a" is used for old people, not objects. For objects or buildings, "viejo/a" or "antiguo/a" are more appropriate.

4. <u>Es</u> mucho frío por la noche. → <u>Hace</u> mucho frío por la noche.

   Explanation: The correct term to describe the weather being cold is "hace frío".

Activity 8

Multiple Choice

1. It's very hot.

   a) Hace mucho calor.

Explanation: "Hace mucho calor" is the standard way to express "It's very hot" in Spanish.

2. The former director is here.

   b) El antiguo director está aquí.

Explanation: "Antiguo" can be used to describe someone's former role or position.

Activity 9

Sentence Creation

1. El libro es muy antiguo.

    Explanation: This sentence indicates that the book is very old.

2. Juan es mi hermano mayor.

    Explanation: This describes Juan as being the older brother.

3. Hace mucho viento hoy.

    Explanation: This sentence indicates that the weather is windy today.

4. Pedro es muy antiguo.

    Explanation: This means Pedro is old-fashioned in his way of thinking/behaving.

Activity 10

Story Error Identification

"Es un día soleado. Hace <u>es</u> calor. Mariana y su hermano <u>más viejo</u>, Carlos, deciden visitar un museo. El museo es muy <u>anciano</u> y tiene muchos artefactos antiguos".

Corrected Version:

"Es un día soleado. <u>Hace</u> calor. Mariana y su hermano <u>mayor</u>, Carlos, deciden visitar un museo. El museo es muy <u>viejo/antiguo</u> y tiene muchos artefactos antiguos".

Explanation:

"Hace es" should be "Hace" to express "it's hot".

"Hermano más viejo" should be "hermano mayor" when referring to an older brother.

"Museo muy anciano" is incorrect because "anciano" is used for people.

Activity 11

Mistake Correction

1. <u>Me jugar fútbol.</u>

   Corrected: Juego fútbol.

   Explanation: The verb "jugar" (to play) is not reflexive, so "me" is not necessary.

2. <u>Me comer pollo.</u>

   Corrected: Como pollo.

   Explanation: The verb "comer" (to eat) is not reflexive, so "me" is not necessary.

3. <u>Me prefiero comer la pizza.</u>

   Corrected: Prefiero comer la pizza.

   Explanation: The verb "preferir" (to prefer) is not reflexive, so "me" is not necessary.

4. <u>Me gusta café porque es sano.</u>

   Corrected: Me gusta el café porque es sano.

   Explanation: In Spanish, when expressing liking for a noun, the definite article (like "el") must be used before the thing we like.

5. <u>Estoy en amor con mi novio.</u>

Corrected: Estoy enamorado/a de mi novio.

Explanation: The correct phrase for being in love in Spanish is "estar enamorado de + person".

The 80 Most Common Mistakes in Spanish

Activity 12

Fill in the Blanks with Reflexive Pronouns

<u>Me</u> llamo Juan.

> Explanation: The reflexive verb "llamarse" is used to mean "to call oneself".

Ellos <u>se</u> visten rápidamente.

> Explanation: The reflexive verb "vestirse" (to dress oneself) requires the pronoun "se" for "ellos".

Tú <u>te</u> bañas cada noche.

> Explanation: The reflexive verb "bañarse" (to bathe oneself) requires the pronoun "te" for "tú".

Nosotros <u>nos</u> peinamos en el baño.

> Explanation: The reflexive verb "peinarse" (to comb oneself) requires the pronoun "nos" for "nosotros".

Activity 13

Translate the Sentences

I like dogs = Me gustan los perros. "Gustan" is used because "perros" is plural and as "perros" is performing the action of "pleasing me" we use the "-an" ending.

I prefer to drink tea = Prefiero beber té. "Preferir" is used to express preference. Remember "me prefiero" is wrong.

He talks to himself = Se habla a sí mismo. The reflexive verb and pronoun are used to indicate the action is performed on oneself.

You like to dance = Te gusta bailar. "Te" is used with "you".

We are in love with the city = Estamos enamorados de la ciudad. "Enamorado de" is the correct phrase for expressing being in love with something.

Activity 14

Matching Activity

Me gusta el té = I like tea.

Te hablo = I talk to you.

Prefiero = I prefer.

Me fascina la música = Music fascinates me.

Activity 15

Gustar Sentences

Here's a sample answer:

1. Me gusta la música clásica.

2. No me gusta el calor extremo.

3. Me gustan las películas de acción.

4. Me gusta leer libros de ciencia ficción.

5. No me gusta comer temprano.

Activity 16

True or False. State if the translation is correct (True) or incorrect (False):

1. He was in the cinema = Estuvo en el cine. <u>True.</u>

2. What is your name? =¿Qué es tu nombre? <u>False.</u> (Correct translation: ¿Cuál es tu nombre?)

3. I had to ask for directions = Tuve que preguntar por direcciones. <u>True.</u>

4. My dad has no beard = Mi padre tiene no barba. <u>False</u>. (Correct translation: Mi padre no tiene barba.)

5. She feels like eating = Siente como comer. <u>False.</u> (Correct translation: Le apetece comer.)

Activity 17

Fill in the Blanks

1. Ayer usé mi móvil para <u>ver</u> vídeos.

2. Me gustaría <u>casarme</u> con alguien especial.

3. Tengo ganas de <u>ir</u> al parque.

4. No sé qué <u>hacer</u> mañana.

5. ¿<u>Estás</u> listo para la reunión?

Activity 18

Translate from English to Spanish.
Translate the following sentences:

1. How are you feeling today = ¿Cómo te sientes hoy?

2. I don't know what to say = No sé qué decir.

3. What is your address? = ¿Cuál es tu dirección?

4. I have to buy a new dress = Tengo que comprar un vestido nuevo.

5. She was at the beach last weekend= Estuvo en la playa el fin de semana pasado.

Activity 19

Fill in the Blanks with "Qué" or "Cuál".

1. ¿Cuál es tu plan para el fin de semana? (asking about a specific plan)

2. ¿Cuál es tu dirección? (asking about your specific address)

3. ¿Qué piensas de la película? (broad question)

4. ¿Cuál es tu color favorito? (specific colour)

5. ¿Cuál es la razón de tu visita? (specfici reason)

The 80 Most Common Mistakes in Spanish

Activity 20

Match the English phrasal verb to its corresponding Spanish verb.

English	Spanish
a) To give up	2) Abandonar
b) To run	1) Correr
c) To look for	5) Buscar
d) To look	3) Mirar
e) To run out	4) Acabarse

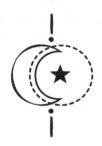

Activity 21

Decide which version of the sentence is correct.

1. Ellos son 16 años.
2. <u>Ellos tienen 16 años.</u>

    Explanation: In Spanish, age is expressed using the verb "tener" (to have).

1. <u>Me gusta el vino blanco.</u>
2. Me gusta vino blanco.

    Explanation: When we use an opinion expression we must use "the" with the noun.

1. Mi hermano está embarazado.
2. <u>Mi hermano está avergonzado.</u>

    Explanation: "Embarazado" means "pregnant for males". The right word for "embarrassed" is "avergonzado".

1. Tengo frío en mis pies.
2. <u>Tengo frío en los pies.</u>

Explanation: In Spanish, when referring to parts of the body, it's common to use the definite article (los, las) rather than the possessive (mis, tus).

1. Hago pocos errores cuando hablo español.

2. <u>Tengo pocos errores cuando hablo español.</u>

   Explanation: In Spanish, we don't "make mistakes", we "have" them.

Activity 22

Fill in the Blanks

1. Me duele <u>la</u> cabeza. Explanation: Again, when referring to parts of the body, "the" is used in Spanish rather than "my".

2. Mi móvil no <u>funciona</u>. Explanation: "Funcionar" is the correct verb to use when something is not working.

3. Tengo un montón de <u>diversión</u>. Explanation: When talking about having fun as a noun, we use "diversión".

4. Cuanto más <u>estudias</u>, más <u>aprendes</u>. Explanation: It is the combination that makes more sense.

5. Ayer <u>tuve</u> un montón de diversión en la fiesta. (tuve/tenía). Explanation: "Tuve" is the preterite form, indicating a specific past event. "Tenía" means "I used to have".

The 80 Most Common Mistakes in Spanish

Activity 23

Correct the Mistakes

1. Estamos esperando <u>por</u> la comida.

    Corrected: Estamos esperando la comida.

    Explanation: "Esperar" doesn't need a preposition in this context.

2. Fui a Italia dos <u>tiempos</u> este verano.

    Corrected: Fui a Italia dos <u>veces</u> este verano.

    Explanation: We use "veces" to denote frequency or "times".

3. Me duelen <u>mis</u> manos.

    Corrected: Me duelen <u>las</u> manos.

    Explanation: We use "the" in Spanish with body parts.

4. Ayer tuve un montón de <u>divertido</u>.

    Corrected: Ayer tuve un montón de <u>diversión</u>.

    Explanation: "Divertido" is an adjective. For the noun form, we use "diversión".

Activity 24

Translate into Spanish

1. My phone doesn't work = Mi móvil no funciona. "Funciona" is the verb for something working.

2. The more I read, the more I understand = Cuanto más leo, más entiendo. This follows the "cuanto más X más Y" structure.

3. My head hurts = Me duele la cabeza. When referring to parts of the body, it's common to use the definite article (los, las) rather than the possessive (mis, tus).

4. I'm waiting for my friend = Estoy esperando a mi amigo. Explanation: When waiting for a person, we use the preposition "a".

5. My feet are cold = Tengo frío en los pies. "Tener frío" means "to be cold". We specify the body part with "en" and use "los" rather than "mis".

Activity 25

Fun with False Friends

1. **Embarazada:** Pregnant (A common false friend. It does not mean embarrassed).

2. **Diversión:** Fun (It refers to amusement or entertainment).

3. **Actualmente:** Currently (It does not mean "actually". It refers to the present time).

4. **Asistir:** To attend (It does not mean "assist". It means to be present at an event).

5. **Sano:** Healthy (It refers to health or being in good condition).

Activity 26

Choose the Correct Translation

My teacher wants me to practise more.

   a) Mi profesor quiere yo practico más.
   b) <u>Mi profesor quiere que practique más.</u>

   Explanation: In Spanish, when expressing someone's wish or desire for another person to do something, we use the subjunctive form after "que".

She called her brother lazy.

   a) <u>Ella llamó perezoso a su hermano.</u>
   b) Ella llamó un perezoso a su hermano.

   Explanation: In Spanish, we don't use "a" (un) in this kind of structure.

Be careful when walking on the street.

   a) Ten cuidado cuando caminando en la calle.
   b) <u>Ten cuidado cuando camines por la calle.</u>

Explanation: In Spanish, we use the present tense (subjunctive) form of the verb after "cuando" to express actions that are not yet completed.

I know a man who can help you.

> a) Conozco a un hombre quien puede ayudarte.
>
> <u>b) Conozco a un hombre que puede ayudarte.</u>

> Explanation: In Spanish, we use "que" after the noun to introduce relative clauses that provide additional information about the noun. We normally use "quien" when we have "con" (with).

You look tired.

> <u>a) Pareces cansado.</u>
>
> b) Estás cansado.

> Explanation: Both options would express a similar message but the first one has an emphasis on the external look: you look tired to me but you might not necesarilly be so (which estás cansado implies).

Activity 27

Fill in the Blanks

1. Mi prima quiere que yo (<u>cante</u>/canta) en la boda. The correct form of the verb "cantar" in the subjunctive tense is "cante".

2. Mi amigo me llamó (<u>tonto</u>/un tonto). In Spanish, we omit "a" (un) in this sort of structure.

3. Siempre sonríe cuando (trabajando/<u>trabaja</u>) con niños. In this context, the correct form is the present tense (trabaja) as "trabajando" wouldn't make sense unless we add "está trabajando".

4. Ella es la chica con (<u>quien</u>/que) salí ayer. Explanation: In this case we use "quien" as we have the preposition "with".

5. Hoy (eres/<u>estás</u>) muy feliz. Explanation: In this sentence we would choose "estás" as we have "hoy" indicating a temporary state of things, not a permanent one which "eres" would imply.

The 80 Most Common Mistakes in Spanish

Activity 28

True or False

1. My friend wants me to come early. -> Mi amigo quiere que venga temprano. <u>True</u>.

Explanation: In Spanish, when expressing someone's wish or desire for another person to do something, we use the subjunctive form after "que".

2. He called me a genius. -> Él me llamó un genio. <u>False</u>.

Explanation: In Spanish, we don't use the article "a" when saying that someone insulted/called someone something. We would omit also "él" unless we want to emphasise that it was him (and not her). Therefore, we would say "Me llamó genio".

3. Be careful when driving at night. -> Ten cuidado cuando conduciendo de noche. <u>False</u>.

Explanation: In Spanish, we use the present tense (subjunctive) form of the verb after "cuando" to express actions that are not yet completed.

4. That's the guy who helped me. -> Ese es el chico quien me ayudó. <u>False</u>.

Explanation: In this case, we don't have the preposition "with" (con) in the sentence, so therefore we can't use "quien".

5. You look upset. -> Pareces molesto. <u>True</u>.

Explanation: In this context, "pareces" is used to express the temporary state of looking a certain way. We could also ask by saying: "¿Estás molesto?".

Activity 29

Match up the sentences

My cousin would like me to visit her.	A mi prima le gustaría que la visite.
She called me intelligent.	Me llamó inteligente.
I'm always happy when singing.	Siempre estoy feliz cuando canto.
She is the person with whom I spoke.	Ella es la persona con quién hablé.
You look fantastic.	Estás fantástico.

Activity 30

**Sentence Correction. Correct the mistakes
in the following Spanish sentences:**

I. Mi jefe quiere yo <u>trabajar</u> más tarde. -> Mi jefe quiere
<u>que</u> yo <u>trabaje</u> más tarde.

Explanation: The mistake was using "quiere yo"
instead of "quiere que". In Spanish, when expressing
someone's desire or request, we use "querer que"
followed by the subjunctive form of the verb. Also
we use the subjunctive in this structure as it is a wish.

2. Mi hermana me llamó bonita <u>a mí</u>. -> Mi hermana
me llamó bonita.

Explanation: The mistake was using "a mí" at the
end of the sentence. In Spanish, it's not necessary
to include "a mí" in this context because the subject
is clear from the sentence structure.

3. Cuida tus pasos cuando <u>corriendo</u>. -> Cuida tus
pasos cuando <u>corras</u>.

Explanation: The mistake was using "corriendo"
instead of "corras". The correct form should be
the infinitive form "corras" to match the structure
"cuando + verb" (when + verb).

4. Él es el chico <u>quien</u> me vendió el coche. -> Él es el chico <u>que</u> me vendió el coche.

   Explanation: The mistake was using "quien" instead of "que". In Spanish, "que" is used as the relative pronoun to introduce defining clauses, indicating who or what is being referred to. Note that we don't have the preposition "with" (con) in the sentence so we must use "que".

5. Hoy <u>eres</u> muy animado. -> Hoy <u>estás</u> muy animado/a.

   Explanation: We use "estar" to convey that today you look really happy/lively.

About the Author

I'm Fran García, serving as the Head of Spanish at a secondary school in London. I teach Spanish and French. I am also a GCSE examiner for AQA and Edexcel. I am an Official Spanish Examiner, authorised by the Instituto Cervantes. I completed my BA in Philosophy at the University of Murcia, including a year abroad at the University of Hull. Additionally, I pursued studies at Sheffield Hallam University and the University of Sheffield. My teaching experience spans across Spain, the UK, and India. My curiosity persists, akin to that of a child, and I strive to keep that flame alive.

Traveling ranks among my greatest pleasures. If I were to pick favourite sports, swimming and cycling would be at the top of my list. I also have a passion for music, art, and reading.

Having transitioned from Philosophy into the realm of languages, my aspiration is to delve into the intricacies of linguistic mechanisms. While I hold a fondness for philosophy, I chose languages as my profession due to the perpetual learning and improvement they offer each day, even if it's just a new word. This served as a compelling motivation for me.

I trust my book serves you well, its content proving both valuable and aesthetically pleasing, guiding you a bit further along the beautiful yet challenging journey of language acquisition.

Should you wish to contact me, feel free to do so at dubois.francisco@gmail.com.

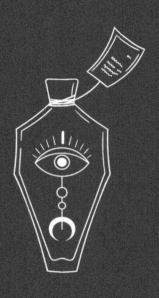